PATTERNS OVER TIME
A Research Summary

Screen Time &
Healthy Development

By Gloria DeGaetano, M.Ed.
Founder/CEO Parent Coaching Institute

Kudos for *Patterns Over Time*

"Gloria DeGaetano's new book, *Patterns Over Time*, researches the effects of screen time (smart phones, computers, television, etc.) on childhood development. This book is important, timely, well-researched, and fully accessible. It assists parents in guiding their developing child in the proper use of screen time, fostering its benefits and ameliorating the negative effects of excessive and inappropriate screen time usage. Highly recommended."

~ Robert Numan, PhD, Emeritus Professor of Behavioral Neuroscience, Santa Clara University

"This piece of work that Gloria has brilliantly synthesized looks at highly pertinent and critical angles of screen time and healthy development that parents are not likely to have had the opportunity to consider yet. The profound insights Gloria shares here are a 'must read' for all parents, educators and professionals in the child/teen space."

~ Fiona Emwanu, PCI Certified Parent Coach®, Parents Looking Forward
www.parentslookingforward.co.za
Johannesburg, South Africa

"Children are spending an unprecedented amount of time with screens, and suffering for it: depression, anxiety, aggression, loss of social connection, sexualization are all on the rise. This timely book is a must-read for parents, educators, or anyone who works with children."

~ Melissa Henson, Program Director, Parents and Television and Media Council
www.parentstv.org

"Living in Silicon Valley for over 40 years, I have painfully witnessed the invasion of screens into both the lives of parents, as well as their children. It's impossible to go out to dinner and not be seated next to a table of family members, connecting with their individual screens rather than each other, wasting what for families in the past used to be a golden opportunity for honest and open communication. Gloria is a renowned parent coach and brilliant communicator who, for decades, has been a world leader in raising the alarm about how screens are destroying the lives of our children. In *Patterns Over Time*, she clearly presents the findings of evidence-based research to encourage parents to re-evaluate the values that undergird their lives and make choices that affirm their love and connectedness to their children, rather than allowing screens to seize control of their parenting journey."

~ Lea Stublarec, MSW, PCI Certified Parent Coach®, Gifted Daughters,
www.GiftedDaughters.com
Menlo Park, CA

"In *Patterns Over Time*, Gloria DeGaetano presents a wealth of research about the harmful effects of excessive screen use on children's developing minds, emotions, and bodies while encouraging parents to reduce their children's screen time to promote greater self-awareness, resilience, and healthy development. This book is a vital resource for our time."

~ Diane Dreher, PhD, www.dianedreher.com
Professional Certified Coach and best-selling author of *The Tao of Inner Peace and The Tao of Personal Leadership*

"Gloria DeGaetano, media and parenting guru, takes the reader on a mystical journey starting with television and traveling to screens of all shapes and sizes. *Patterns Over Time* is a one-stop anthology on how the digital world has shaped every aspect of life for children and families. From language and literacy to critical thinking and emotional intelligence, complex cognitive processes are explained through simple but critical interactions of everyday life. Gloria outlines the sometimes-painful truths that parents need to know. But she doesn't leave it there. She provides hope—hope for creating new patterns starting now."

~ Jean Rogers, M.S. Ed., Director, Screen Time Action Network at Fairplay

"*Patterns Over Time* is a uniquely valuable resource for parents, teachers and child service workers. Gloria DeGaetano, Founder and CEO of the Parent Coaching Institute, pulls together in three succinct chapters the very best of recent research findings on the impact of screens and social media in areas of cognitive and emotional development, as well as general health and happiness. The information is laid out in an easily accessible format, and the sometimes obscure, jargon of academic research is masterfully translated into the language of the parental community. Packed full with learning and wisdom, this short book will be a go-to reference for many years to come."

~ Daniel Liechty, PhD., D.Min., ACSW, LCSW, Professor of Social Work, Illinois State University

"This incredible, intelligent and insightful work needs to be read by every person that uses a personal device such as an iPhone or tablet. Not just parents. The future of our social interactions, our ability to make decisions, our ability to problem solve, and our ability to use our brains are crumbling before our eyes as we are sucked into the world of the screen. This is a horror movie in the making. And we are making it every day ourselves—every time we pick up our devices. Gloria DeGaetano predicted this years ago to closed ears. We are now seeing the results in our children. Her forecast was correct and she has been screaming a "Call to Action" that everyone of us needs to listen to and make choices that our iPhones have nothing to do with."

~ Vanessa Haycock, NTS, LMP, CCHT,
www.vanessahaycock.com

TABLE OF CONTENTS

Introduction

On a walk one sunny morning I passed a young man who smiled and announced a cheerful, "Good Morning." I was just about to respond "Good Morning" back to him when I noticed he wasn't looking at me but off in the distance. I quickly realized: The greeting wasn't for me. He was talking to someone on his cell phone. So, I kept silent. One block later I encountered a mom pushing her toddler in a stroller. From his perch the boy initiated a friendly wave with his chubby hand. Cuteness personified! Then he beamed his clear blue eyes right into mine while offering the sweetest, slightly shy smile. I waved back, smiling, wishing him and his mom a good morning. Mom and I exchanged those knowing smiles mothers everywhere immediately translate. "You have one sweet precious bundle," my smile told her. "I know and thank you," her smile told me. No words were necessary for this poignant human connection.

Continuing walking, my initial energy from this encounter waned as I thought: Will this little boy grow up with his nose in his phone, oblivious to the people around him? Or will he continue to smile and seek to connect with his fellow humans? As an adult will he use screens (and who knows what other forms of technology by then?) for human purposes that enhance his life, the life of others, and life in general?

The answer, of course, is: It depends. Whether a child becomes an adult who uses technology with life in mind and human connection prioritized depends on screen time habits formed and practiced daily throughout childhood and the teen years. Whether or not real-world interactions will

Whether or not time with screens wallops the will to spend time in other human activities depends on a lot of factors.

take precedence over screen-mediated ones may also depend on what children learn to value early on. And, certainly, where they put their attention during the multitude of experiences from birth to young adulthood, will affect what they value.

How they grow up answering questions like: "What is most meaningful to you? How do you know?" will significantly shape media/digital habits. Then there's how resilient kids become to be able to withstand peer and societal pressure to be on screens eight or more hours every day.

We can safely say that whether or not time with screens wallops the will to spend time in other human activities depends on a lot of factors.

In our screen-saturated world, training kids to use digital devices as intentional tools in service of their optimal growth, rather than as thoughtless tethers that truncate their development, takes a lot of time, effort, energy and patience on the part of parents and caregivers. And unfortunately, yet understandably, these are usually in short supply as adults fight their own demons to control and manage their screen use. Current research indicates parents use digital media (e.g., television, computers, smartphones, tablets) an average of 9 hours per day,[1] with more than three hours a day on their smartphones.[2] Some studies show that American adults spend an average of 5 hours a day browsing on their cell phones, touching it with a tap, swipe, or click an average of 2,617 times per day![3]

In a 2018 study that examined associations between maternal mobile device use with the frequency mothers interacted with their 6-year-olds, it was found that mothers with device use initiated fewer verbal and nonverbal interactions with their children than mothers who did not use a device.[4] In another study of families' mobile device use, patterns revealed that children are often frustrated by the sudden withdrawal of parental attention when responding to a notification on a mobile device, especially if the reason for device use is unclear to the child. This study also revealed that parents sometime use mobile devices as a way to actively withdraw from parenting duties— pretending to be occupied with something important when children need help—the moms and dads interviewed considered this as a "desirable disengagement" to find time for oneself amid parenting demands.[5] In another six-month 2018 study of 183 couples, researchers found that parents use digital technology devices as a potential means of escape and for stress management with their children from birth through age 5. And because of the bi-directionality of the technology interference and parent-child interactions, it was found that increased mobile device use by parents increased child tantrums and uncooperative behaviors. The authors concluded, "Our results suggest bidirectional dynamics in which (a) parents, stressed by their child's difficult behavior, may then withdraw from parent–child interactions with technology and (b) this higher technology use during parent–child interactions may influence externalizing and withdrawal behaviors of the children over time."[6]

Since too much screen time plays havoc with the parent-child bond, with parents' locus of attention and their ability to tend in timely ways to children's needs and because parent media use is a strong predictor of the child's media/digital habits, much is to be gained when parents limit their own screen use.[7]

The parents I coach want to limit their own screen use and screen use for their children, knowing that too much screen time, "isn't good for kids." But they are usually stymied by two questions:

- How much is too much screen time for my child/teen? And…

- Can too much screen time negatively affect my child/teen? If so, how?

Let's consider each question below.

HOW MUCH IS TOO MUCH SCREEN TIME?

Once again, the appropriate limits for screen use will depend on several factors. The age and maturity of the child certainly play a critical role. As does the type of content absorbed. Whether or not the parent or a caring adult discusses the content with the child determines how the screen experience affects the child. And we can expect that the influencing factors for one child won't be the same for another child. In fact, we probably know children in the same family who are affected differently by too much screen time!

There are well-established guidelines by experts, that if applied by parents, would reduce potential negative effects and increase the likelihood of screen time being supportive of optimal development—for most children and teens.

Considering all the valid variables, however, there are well-established guidelines by experts, that if applied by parents, would reduce potential negative effects and increase the likelihood of screen time being supportive of optimal development—for most children and teens.

Screen Time Recommendations for Children Birth-Age 5

The American Academy of Pediatrics (AAP) identifies guidelines for young children in a 2016 policy statement:

"For children younger than 18 months, discourage use of screen media other than video-chatting."

"Evidence is sufficient to recommend time limitations on digital media use for children 2 to 5 years to no more than 1 hour per day to allow children ample time to engage in other activities important to their health and development and to establish media viewing habits associated with lower risk of obesity later on."

And they further encourage parents: "For children 2 to 5 years of age, limit screen use to 1 hour per day of high-quality programming, co-view with your children, help children understand what they are seeing, and help them apply what they learn to the world around them."[8]

The American Academy of Child and Adolescent Psychiatry recommends: "Avoid using screens as pacifiers, babysitters, or to stop tantrums."[9]

And The World Health Organization (WHO) has issued clear guidelines—to "sit less and play more."

"For one year and younger, sedentary screen time is not recommended. For those aged 2-5 years, sedentary screen time should be no more than 1 hour; less is better. When sedentary, engaging in reading and storytelling with a caregiver is encouraged."[10]

Screen Time Recommendations For Children Ages 6 and Older (Including Teens)

The American Academy of Child and Adolescent Psychiatry doesn't provide a specific time limit but highly recommends:

- For ages 6 and older, encourage healthy habits and limit activities that include screens.
- Turn off all screens during family meals and outings.
- Learn about and use parental controls.
- Turn off screens and remove them from bedrooms 30-60 minutes before bedtime.[11]

The American Academy of Pediatrics (AAP) provides similar advice:

"For children ages 6 years and older, set media use limits that factor in other health-promoting activities such as physical activity, sleep, family meals, school and friends."[12] They strongly encourage families to come up with a Media Plan that will set clear limits and expectations for screen time and use. They provide resources for doing so on their website.

In their policy statement, "Media Use in School-Aged Children and Adolescents," AAP's Council on Communication and Media state, "The effects of media use are multifactorial and depend on the type of media, the type of use, the amount and extent of use, and the characteristics of the individual child.

Children today are growing up in an era of highly personalized media use experiences, so parents must develop personalized media use plans for their children that attend to each child's age, health, temperament, and developmental stage. Research evidence shows that children and teenagers need adequate sleep, physical activity, and time away from media."[13]

Which brings us to our second question…

Knowing the research empowers us to make decisions aligned with what we believe is best for our kids.

CAN TOO MUCH SCREEN TIME NEGATIVELY AFFECT MY CHILD/TEEN? IF SO, HOW?

I compiled this book to answer this question. I wanted to give you an overview of the research so that you can see quite readily that over time—**yes, too much screen time can negatively impact children's and teens' development.** I arranged this vital information in three major categories.

Too Much Screen Time's Impact on:

- Thinking and Learning
- Feelings and Behavior
- General Health and Well Being

It's important to keep in mind that the evidence from one research study on a certain topic is limited and can't give us adequate information to take effective actions. Therefore, I have included several studies on specific topics —and as often as I could, I cited longitudinal studies over many years or even decades. *Distinct similar patterns from studies spanning time give clearer indications of potential effects.* And can spur decisions aligned with what is most important and meaningful to us.

This book concentrates on the research findings. Knowing the research empowers us to make decisions aligned with what we believe

is best for our kids. And interestingly, the research findings here naturally turn us in the direction of positive solutions. Many are simple solutions—such as helping kids spend more time exercising, or more time in Nature, or reading every day. **Indeed, a comprehensive review of the research literature suggests that the long-term implications of digital technology use depend on the type of activities it displaces.**[14]

Reduce screen time and naturally there is more time to include varied real-life experiences in a day, a week—throughout the years of your child's/teen's development.

While it is easy to say, "Just make sure your kids do more in the real-world than they do on screens," we both know it's incredibly challenging to make this happen on a consistent basis. And understandably so. In our digitally-driven society, moms and dads need large, on-going supplies of determination, stamina, and conviction to limit screen time and require kids to spend more time in 3-D reality. These are often in short-supply as parents must battle Big Tech's stranglehold on our kids, both kids' and adult peer pressure and

In our digitally-driven society, moms and dads need large, on-going supplies of determination, stamina, and conviction to limit screen time and require kids to spend more time in 3-D reality.

school mandates for increased use of screens in education—to name a few of today's unprecedented parenting challenges.

Limiting screen time so children and teens can come to greater understanding of themselves through personal interactions and varied experiences in the real world is the first step. The second step is to mediate children's and teens' screen experiences to ensure regular exposure to quality content. Showing and stressing the ways kids can learn from educational games, apps, documentaries, for instance, can guide them to use all forms of technology wisely. I encourage the parents I work with to

11

also observe the nuances of behaviors and attitudes their children and teens exhibit around all forms of screen devices. This sets the stage for exploring how kids perceive themselves as in-control users of technology and often brings up interesting talking points that key in on media/digital literacy skills. As you read the following research, please keep in mind that modern-day patterns of screen use with mobile, connected devices or interactive games and apps, are obviously different from passively watching television or relaxing with a movie. Yet, both types of processes hold challenges for ensuring optimal development. And, conversely, both types can certainly be used to effectively train children and teens to be wise, creative users of all forms of "screen machines." In this compilation, I have included both passive and interactive screen-use research so that you can consider how you might want to approach both in your family or with the parents you serve.

Ideally parents today would accomplish **two goals:**

1. **Limit the quantity of screen exposure** so that their children and teens enjoy a wide variety of personal interactions and enriching experiences in the natural world, appropriate to their age and stage of development.

2. **Attend to the quality of engagement with quality screen content** so that children and teens think critically about what they do with any form of screen technology, as well as why they do it, what they learn from it, and how screen interactions and the screen content they choose helps them become better people.

If these are your goals, I know the information here can help. It gives you solid reasons to take actions appropriate for your child's/teen's well-being. It affirms educational choices for quality content and confirms your important role as guide, mediator, and teacher to grow your children optimally in these technological times.

After all, we can't wait for research "to prove" too much screen time is not harmful. Only you can decide through your deep knowledge of your unique child, through your wise observations, and intuitive knowing what's best. So, as you read the research findings on the following pages, please keep that in mind, and in your heart.

CHAPTER 1

Impact on Thinking and Learning

DECREASED ATTENTION SPAN

A habit of fast-paced television or video or app games keeps children's attention restricted according to the pace of the production. But, when children are engaged in other activities, attention is dependent upon the task at hand and is largely determined internally by the child's choices and desires. When youngsters make choices in self-directed play, or when older kids do their homework, for instance, they are also talking to themselves, guiding their attention internally to focus on one thing and then another. They are choosing what to attend to and when to shift their attention— no one is doing it for them.

Passive screen time limits self-talk.

Children watching without any adult guidance are not saying much to themselves about what to pay attention to or explaining to themselves about what is more important than something else.

Child does not choose what to focus on.

The producers, scriptwriters, app and video game makers decide how long children and teens should focus on one thing. The child's attention span is continually interrupted by the shifts of images which occur on TV, on average every 3-5 seconds. However, in a three-dimensional environment, (real life!) children quite naturally spend larger chunks of time focused on one thing at a time, practicing giving attention and developing their attention spans in the process.

Child cannot easily engage in a thinking process.

The constant stream of the rapid changes of images do not allow for higher level thinking processes to occur. Indeed, they can't occur since the cortex, the thinking function of the brain, takes more time to respond than 3-5 seconds, usually 7-10 seconds. A constant diet of fast-paced images can, over time, actually wear out the developing attention span. The cortex basically says, "What's the use?" to try to pay attention to such fast-paced visual data coming in. Research conducted by Peter Jensen concluded, "Extensive exposure to television and video games may promote development of brain systems that scan and shift attention at the expense of those that focus attention."[1]

13

Because sense cannot readily be made of the fast-paced incoming information, frustration sets in and the cortex gives up trying to understand. If this occurrence becomes a daily habit, the child's cortex gets conditioned to be "lazy" in the face of incoming data perceived as indecipherable. This is one of the basic reasons that children who watch a lot of TV have a difficult time sustaining self-directed exploration in any form. The weakened attention span combined with a cortex that has difficulty accepting challenges results in youngsters who hold back or who "don't know how to play" or "who can't focus long enough to learn how to read."

The "weakened attention" span likely derives from sub-cortical areas of the brain that are not growing optimally because of weakened modulation through lack of experiences that require focused attention. Amire Raz and Jason Buhle have done an extensive review of

"Commercial television, with its clever use of constantly changing short sequences, holds our attention by a sensory bombardment that maximizes orienting responses.... TV trains us to watch it."

the research on the brain's attentional networks. They point out, "Cortical and sub-cortical networks mediate different aspects of attention; without the modulatory influence of sub-cortical areas, the brain would not attend effectively."[2]

However, with opportunities to focus and "intentionally attend," children's attention spans develop and deepen. Raz and Buhle go on to say that "as neuroimaging begins to unravel the effects of practice on brain substrates, cumulative findings suggest that the attentional networks can be modified. Introducing attentional training in preschools or childcare centers could be an educational innovation."[3]

Because children are looking at the screen does not mean they are paying attention to the screen. Anderson and his colleagues conducted research in which children were observed watching many different types of television shows. A significant conclusion was, "a child is increasingly likely to continue to look at the TV the longer the look progresses. If a look lasts longer than about 15 seconds, the child has a strong tendency to become progressively 'locked in' to the TV screen."[4]

This tendency toward attentional inertia is what many parents experience as a zoned-out effect in their children when placed in front of a screen. Their brains are not actively engaged with the mental demands needed to give focused attention. In fact, often their entire bodies reflect a passive trance-like quality. The researchers in the above study noted, "If a look continued beyond about 10 seconds, we often observed the child's body relax, head slouch forward, and mouth drop open."[5]

The complex factors involved with the saliency of the quick changes to hook a child's orienting response increase the frequency of looking and impede the development of selective attention brain functions. Dr. Jerome Singer, a former researcher on children and television at Yale University has famously said:

"Commercial television, with its clever use of constantly changing short sequences, holds our attention by a sensory bombardment that maximizes orienting responses. We are constantly drawn back to the set and to processing each new sequence of information as it is presented. TV trains us to watch it."[6]

This entrained reaction becomes even more significant when we consider that children younger than two years old are increasingly watching television and DVDs. Zimmerman and his team at the University of Washington surveyed over 1,000 parents in Minnesota and Washington State. Their findings are startling, considering the fact that the American Academy of Pediatrics strongly recommends no television viewing or screen exposure for children younger than two years of age. The parents in this study reported that by three months of age, about 40% of children regularly watched television, DVDs, or videos. By 24 months, this proportion rose to 90%. The median age at which regular media exposure was introduced was nine months. The average viewing time per day rose from one hour per day for children younger than 12 months to more than 1.5 hours per day by 24 months.[7]

In another study, Zimmerman and his colleagues found that the association between early television viewing and subsequent attentional problems is specific to non-educational viewing and to viewing before age three. There

is a significant association between early TV viewing before the age of three and subsequent attention problems at age seven.[8]

Indeed, several cross-sectional studies found that preschool viewing of quality programming *without* commercials was positively associated with measures of attention and executive control, whereas viewing similar content *with* commercials correlated with poor performance.[9] These findings suggest that the presence of commercial breaks require children to constantly disengage and re-engage their attention to the screen, promoting a reactive style of attention and making it particularly difficult for young viewers to link concepts together and extract meaning from programming. This could become problematic in that subscription-based screen content may provide kids with no or little commercial content in the short-term, but in the long term could lead to increased socio-economic (SES) disparities in attention as a result.[10]

Overall, long-term studies show that young children are especially susceptible to fast-paced screen content. In a 2019 longitudinal Canadian study, Tamana and associates found that when preschoolers were exposed to 2 or more hours a day of TV, it worsened their attention spans.[11] An added dimension to this issue is that time with screens may be limiting the cortex's actual capacity to pay attention. In PET scan studies, Dr. Douglas Gentile, from Iowa State University, showed that technology use of greater than 5 hours per day was consistent with neurological "pruning" of tracks to the frontal cortex, important for executive functioning and impulse control.[12]

A longitudinal study conducted by Landuis and his colleagues observed that the mean of hours of television viewing during childhood was associated with symptoms of attention problems in adolescence. These associations remained significant after controlling for gender, attention problems in early childhood, cognitive ability at five years of age, and childhood socioeconomic status. This association was also independent of adolescent television viewing. The researchers concluded that too much childhood television viewing, over two hours daily, can contribute to the development of attention problems and suggest that the effects may be long-lasting.[13] Some researchers believe iPad use in young children could even be more deleterious: "With iPad use, children are exposed to continuously shifting and interactive stimuli that drive and direct their attention.

Childhood attention problems give way to teen attention problems. Research demonstrates that youth who spend more time playing video games have more attention problems, and those who are more impulsive or have more attention problems subsequently spend more time playing video games.

Because of the numerous exogenous interactive stimuli and constantly changing visual stimulation in iPad apps and games, children may not develop the ability to inhibit visual distracters, and thus face problems in the development of focused visual spatial attention span in circumstances without rapid exogenous stimulation."[14]

Childhood attention problems give way to teen attention problems. Research demonstrates that youth who spend more time playing video

games have more attention problems, and those who are more impulsive or have more attention problems subsequently spend more time playing video games.[15]

These results were replicated in a 2012 study at Iowa State University. In addition, this extensive study found that watching videos on a computer and multi-tasking were related to attention problems. And that the frequency of sending and receiving text messages (but not actual phone conversations) also increases attention problems. Other forms of media use, however, such as listening to music and reading print media, were unrelated to attention problems, since music audio do not involve a screen and print media require much more self-directed (as opposed to stimulus driven) attention.[16]

However, screens on as "background noise" can disrupt young children's play scenarios and school-age children's focus on homework, as well as the quality of parent-child interactions, shifting children's attention to what is on the screen. A daily habit of this continual changing of attention conditions young brains to become easily distracted.[17] (See charts on pages 30 and 34.)

UNDERDEVELOPED OR DELAYED LANGUAGE ABILITIES AND LITERACY SKILLS

The more television is watched in the home, the less family conversation occurs. In fact, in every society into which television has been introduced, there has been a subsequent decrease in the time devoted to socializing.[18] With less socialization comes decreased models for language development for children and teens, less time in expressive modes, and less attention on the importance and emotional necessity of connecting through language with our fellow humans.

Reading time suffers as well. Research conducted in 15 countries shows unequivocally that the amount of time devoted to reading of every sort (books, magazines, newspapers, etc.) declines rapidly as people spend more and more time watching television.[19]

In addition to the amount of reading, reading abilities are also affected with overuse of TV. In the classic studies of three remote Canadian towns, researchers looked at the impact of the introduction of television on reading skills. The Notel town had no television, the Unitel town had only one channel and the Multitel had several channels. In other respects, these towns, and the people in them, were very much the same, differing only in the amount of television available. The results of this study showed that children's reading scores correlated inversely with the amount of television available in the three towns: Reading scores were highest in Notel, next highest in Unitel, and lowest in Multitel. Eventually cable came to Notel, so a second analysis was done two years after television was introduced there to see if reading scores had changed. Researchers found that the reading scores for children in grades 2 and 3 "deteriorated significantly," but that reading scores for grade 8 students went unchanged.[20]

This finding is in alignment with other studies that show that television, or other forms of screen time, will be most disruptive for the skill of reading for those who are in the process of learning to read.[21] Because younger children have less developed skills, they are more vulnerable to negative effects of too much screen use.

With toddlers and preschoolers spending an average of 3-4 hours a day with mobile digital devices, it's important to address the fact that "children decode, decipher, interpret, transmit and create information visually, verbally and aurally in networked and interlinked ways, long before they are able or required to deal with blocks of print on a static page."[22] In fact, a 2019[23] study as well as a 2020 study[24] demonstrate that, "the transportability, simple user interface and perceived educational value of touch-screen devices means that parents are more likely to use them as part of their daily routine with young children." Consequently, children's current and future linguistic abilities, as well as their brain development, are continually impacted on a daily basis.

Our current societal shift from pencil and paper to the visual screen has been compared to ancient Greeks' shift from oral storytelling to the newer forms of reading and writing. In light of how the human brain functions, this analogy is not at all accurate. The Greeks made a transition from oral language, a brain activity requiring symbolic processing, to written language, another brain activity requiring symbolic processing. Although aspects of long-term memory were lost when the oral tradition was lost, the human cerebral cortex continued to master higher forms of abstract thought and symbolic thinking.

Thinking and language are interwoven within the brain. Without consistent practice in symbolic processing in the form of listening to complex linguistic structures, and in talking, reading, and writing, children and teens cannot develop metaphoric thinking or master higher forms of thinking such as analysis and evaluation. Dr. Jane Healy reminds us, "As a society, we are inviting intellectual mediocrity if we neglect the quality of the language experience of our young. Linguistic passivity for large numbers of children of any age is a recipe for limitation, not only in their individual development but in the cut of our cultural fabric of thought."[25]

This "linguistic passivity" can be experienced by children when the TV is on as background noise. A 2014 study on the effect of background television on the quantity and quality of parental speech directed at toddlers has

found that background TV reduced words per minute, utterances per minute, and number of new words.[26] Other research shows that both the quantity and the quality of parent-child interactions dropped as a result of background TV.[27] The less children and parents talk, the less competent the child grows linguistically.

When families do get together, such as at mealtime, the presence of TV can have negative effects. In a 2017 study of families with children, ages 6-12, the presence of TV was negatively associated with the dietary healthfulness and emotional atmosphere of the meal and the child's overall dietary quality. In addition, it was positively associated with serving fast food for family meals. Those families who were paying attention to the TV had significantly worse meal dietary healthfulness and were more likely to have fast food at family meals compared to those who were not paying attention. However, even if families are not paying attention to the TV, it appears that simply having the TV on as background noise is associated with deleterious outcomes.

The study went on to recommend that families should be given guidance on turning off the TV and making the family meal a time to connect with one another.[28]

Families should be given guidance on turning off the TV and making the family meal a time to connect with one another.

This is wise advice. Even in this age of mobile devices, children from age 8 months onward can be exposed to the background noise of television for up to 5.5 hours daily.[29] It's important to note the images changes on a screen that is in the child's peripheral vision is what draws the brain's orienting response toward the screen. (See charts on pages 30 and 34.) The "orienting response" was discovered by Pavlov in 1927 and explains why we orient to ambulances or fire trucks as soon as we either see or hear them. Disturbances in our visual or aural fields, which differ from our normal expectations of our usual routine, will cause us to become quickly aware of them in order to process them for potential threat. You may have read the research on trauma. Children who witness or experience continual abuse sometimes wear out their orienting responses, because they are ever on the alert for the next expected violent act. As a consequence, they are left continually scanning their environment to assess the degree of danger, since tragically, they have had so little safety and security in their lives. Their low brain mechanisms become hyper vigilant, making it difficult for them to pay attention or concentrate without continual interruption of focus.

Being in front of images that change continuously overloads the orienting response. Do an experiment. In the evening with the lights low, put your head at an angle to a TV, iPad, smart phone, or a computer and watch a children's cartoon, an adult action movie, or a commercial. Turn your head slightly away, with the screen in your peripheral view and try not to look. Try as hard as you can. What did you discover?

In a 2021 study of mothers with their 20–22-month toddlers, it was found that maternal responsiveness and pedagogical behavior decreased during smartphone interruptions.

Most likely that it's nearly impossible not to look. The colorful, quick images are difficult for low brain systems to resist. (An abrupt change in your environment could mean death, remember!) A steady diet of fast-paced images, thousands daily, over the course of years, has a deleterious effect on the young brain's capacity to concentrate, stay focused, and selectively attend to a mental process requiring time and effort. And, of course, it plays havoc with holding a coherent, sustained conversation with a caring adult.

In addition to screen images interrupting parent-child communication, there is a growing body of research that demonstrates parents' smartphone use with the child present also plays a significant factor in reducing and/or interrupting dialogue between parent and child.

In a 2021 study of mothers with their 20–22-month toddlers, it was found that maternal responsiveness and pedagogical behavior decreased during smartphone interruptions.

Interestingly, the children also increased their positive bids for attention in an attempt to repair such interruptions. The authors concluded, "These findings are consistent with a large body of research…demonstrating that smartphone interruptions decreased parenting quality."[30] In a larger 2021 review of 12 studies focused on parent-child "attachment patterns," the authors found, "Disturbances (as a result of smartphone interruptions) in parental sensitivity can have a negative impact on attachment-related interactional processes between parents and children and on child outcomes, such as self-regulatory capacity."[31]

For youngsters to develop self-regulatory capacities, their brain's executive function (EF) needs to be nurtured. Language development supports healthy executive function growth. Unfortunately, too much passive screen time can negatively impact EF development. For instance, a 2021 study found an adverse relationship between passive TV time and brain functional/structural connectivity in typically developing young children, specifically related to neurobiological correlates of reading ability in their executive function.[32] In another 2021 study, results also indicated that when 5-and 6-year-olds spend time passively with screens their ability to process verbal information is negative affected.[33] This study was consistent with previous studies where time exposed to television was a significant predictor of delayed speech development,[34] as well as with data where independent viewing of television by children was a key factor of speech delay.[35] It's important to note that an important 2005 study emphasized that it was not so much television viewing as a whole that negatively affected speech development, as individual programs were associated with the worst vocabulary development and expressive language production.[36]

Dimitri Christakis, pediatric researcher at Children's Hospital and Regional Medical Center in Seattle, reports that children learn vocabulary, as well as other language skills, largely from verbal interactions with their parents. In a study where he used digital recorders on both parents and children in their homes, Dr. Christakis found that adults typically utter approximately 941 words per hour, yet these adult words are almost completely eliminated when television is audible to the child. His research showed that each hour of audible television was associated with significant reductions in child vocalizations, vocalization duration, and conversational turns. On average, each additional hour of television exposure was also associated with a decrease of 770 words the child heard from an adult during the recording session. Since many American households now report having the television always on, even when no one is watching, researchers report these findings have grave implications for language acquisition and therefore perhaps even early brain development.[37]

In any case, learning to listen, talk, read, or write requires different parts of the brain to be fully engaged and operational within more complex thought ranges. Passive viewing and many entertainment games and apps do not require these processes. **They do not put a demand on the child's or teen's brain to slow down and think critically, especially when unmediated by parents or caring adults.** However, when viewing or gaming is accompanied with conversation with an adult guiding the child's thought process, more vocabulary and more complex syntac-

tic structures are used, enabling the child to deepen literacy skills. Conversations with parents and family members, daily reading, a home environment that supports literacy development, and using screens for educational purposes all work synergistically to support growing linguistic abilities.

An important study clarified the role of home media environments, and in particular educational television programs, in improving various literacy skills in 79 kindergarten and 85 first grade students. Specifically, they assessed concepts of print (where a child was shown stimulus and asked specific words, words that rhyme or mean the same, etc.), phonemic awareness and letter – sound correspondence. During the intervention the children were assigned to viewing an educational program or to a control group, who did no viewing. All children who viewed the program during the intervention had better performance in the word recognition task while phonemic awareness increased more in kindergarten children (those with higher reading risk status and viewers of the educational series during the intervention). Furthermore, the home media environment for the children with higher

and literacy in a child. Since early childhood is a critical time for the development of mental functions, and in particular, speech, it is extremely important to enhance the possibilities of this period and use the opportunities for the development of language and literacy skills. The enriching environment in this case will be precisely the active interaction of the child with the environment, primarily social, through parents and peers. And as Vygotsky showed, it is the imitation and use of the cultural model by the child that will give the developmental effect."[39]

UNDERDEVELOPED OR DELAYED CRITICAL THINKING ABILITIES

Failure and discomfort are integral to learning. And the ability to stay with the frustration of being in uncertainty while working through a difficult mental challenge is crucial for developing critical thinking skills. Yet, research shows that screen brains become easily agitated and frustrated when faced with a complex problem. For instance, studies indicate that young children who overuse TV at the expense of other developmentally appropriate activities become elementary school-age children who lack perseverance when faced with a challenging mental task. They lack the ability to resolve complex problems through trial and error, and tend to get extremely frustrated if an immediate solution is not on the horizon. They quickly give up trying to solve the problem. Dr. Jennings Bryant of the University of Alabama has researched this area. Here are some of his observations:

> "One thing we know is that it (TV viewing) reduces what we call vigilance (the ability to stay actively focused on a task). If they watch lots of fast paced programs and then we give them things to do afterwards such as reading or solving complex puzzles, their stick-to-it-iveness is diminished; they're not as willing to

Engaging higher level-thinking skills, such as problem solving, analysis, and evaluation requires that children and teens be able to stay with a mental challenge.

reading risk status was described as less time reading, less enjoyment reading, fewer books available. They also knew fewer sounds and watched more television.[38]

The authors of a 2021 study on young children and language development provide an apt observation:

> "One can single out the fact that a longer television viewing time in children inevitably leads to a decrease in the amount of communication and play with parents and peers. It is communication that creates an enriching environment for the development of speech

stay with the task. Over time, with excessive viewing, you're going to have less vigilant children. This is especially critical for relatively young children—about three to five years seem to be particularly vulnerable times."[40]

Engaging higher level-thinking skills, such as problem solving, analysis, and evaluation requires that children and teens be able to stay with a mental challenge.

As overuse of TV and video impacts this skill, the following are impacted as well:

The ability to explore and discover new ways of thinking about something

When kids navigate their natural surroundings, their thinking functions are in high gear. Engaged fully in sensory data and multiple mental challenges, they learn to utilize possibility thinking, engaging visualization as well as left-brain cognitive functions. Taking in visual images on a two-dimensional, flat screen requires no such brain gymnastics in order to "get it."

Thinking slowly and intentionally

Children with a screen habit soon need the classroom equivalent of "special effects" in order to engage in a thinking process. Unpracticed and unskilled in the slow-moving thinking process required of higher order brain functioning, they soon become bored and unable to process information moving at a realistic pace. This undeveloped capacity, combined with the fact that the cerebral cortex needs time after an initial stimulus to think, creates the habit of giving a quick response in order to end the ordeal of taxing the brain. In normal brain development, youngsters learn to take time to gather their thoughts to produce a desired result.

Active engagement with incoming data

Mental challenges in the 3-D world provide the impetus for brain connections to be made. Dr. Jerry Levy, a bio-psychologist at the University of Chicago states, "I suspect that normal human brains are built to be challenged and that it is only in the face of an adequate challenge that normal bi-hemispheric brain operations are engaged."[41]

As children and teens spend hours passively in front of a screen, they are often not engaged in a variety of higher-level thinking functions such as recalling essential details, understanding motivation, and drawing implicit inferences. Research shows that the earlier a screen time habit begins, the more difficulty the child will have with higher-level thinking functions.[42]

One reason for this is that young children need a variety of brain-challenging experiences that include a linguistic component in order to develop the internal brain structures capable of such thinking skills as recall and inference. Essentially, in order to comprehend screen content in the form of narration it takes:

- A knowledge of exposition of forms or the general structure of stories
- Knowledge and experience of the world
- Knowledge of the structure of screen content and its particular conventions[43]

Therefore, as children and teens spend more and more time with screens, not only are they limiting brain-challenging experiences, they are also involved in a vicious cycle in which they are not comprehending as much of the screen content as they are capable of when their lives are balanced with other activities, such as story-telling and reading.

Young children, especially, can begin a trajectory of school learning problems with screen overuse. Researchers at the University of Michigan found that every additional hour of TV exposure among toddlers correspond to a future decrease in classroom engagement and success at math, along with increased victimization by classmates.[44]

Students who have television on in the background while doing homework develop fewer skills and retain less information than those who do not.[45] A seminal research compilation supported this finding and showed that heavy TV viewers (i.e., children in 3rd through 6th grade who watch four or more hours per day) spend less effort on schoolwork, have poorer reading skills, play less well with friends, and have fewer hobbies and activities than light viewers.[46] The study concluded that children who are heavy screen users read little, have more attention problems, and poorer language abilities. More recent studies have supported these conclusions.[47] Television and video game use during the middle school years is associated with a negative impact on school performance.[48] Children with the lowest grades spent more time playing video games and less time reading then those with the best grades.[49]

It's also important to note the relationship between physical activity and cortical development.

A 2020 research study looked at the dynamic and nonlinear association between screen time, executive function (EF), and fundamental motor skills (FMS) in preschoolers. Analysis demonstrated that heavy screen time negatively impacted preschoolers' sustained attention executive function capabilities while lack of physical activity (being sedentary with the devices) was a major contributing factor, since "cognition and motor aspects share the same brain basis." The study concluded, "that screen time is intensely associated with executive function and fundamental motor skills."[50]

A 2019 study of preschoolers' brains indicated that those who sat and watched TV more than the recommended amount of one hour daily were insufficient in "white matter." That is, brain scans showed the degree of myelination of the neurons, the coating of the connections between nerve cells with a fatty white substance — myelin — was compromised in youngsters with excessive screen exposure. These children had lower measures of structural integrity and myelination. The results of the cognitive tests correlated well with the children's screen expo-

Young children, especially, can begin a trajectory of school learning problems with screen overuse.

sure; the children with higher screen exposure had poorer expressive language and did worse on tests of language processing speed, like rapidly naming objects. Dr. John S. Hutton, the director of the Reading and Literacy Discovery Center at Cincinnati Children's Hospital and lead author of the study concluded: "Tablets in particular, may be so powerful and encompassing, that they may not belong in the hands of infants-toddlers-preschoolers."[51]

Previous studies, some from longitudinal research, support similar findings of deleterious associations described in young children.[52][53][54]

The more time spent with screens, the greater the risks cognitively—not only in young children, but older children as well. An on-going major study of 10,000 children and teens released results of 4,500 children, ages 8-11, in 2018. Initial findings showed that those who spent more than two hours a day using screens scored lower on language and thinking tests. The average amount of time spent was 3.6 hours daily. Some children with more than

seven hours a day of screen time also experienced thinning of the brain's cortex, the area related to critical thinking and reasoning. It is interesting to note that less screen time was linked to better memory and performance on various cognitive tasks for this age group.[55]

This should give us pause because on a typical day, children spend 4-6 hours and teens up to 9 hours in front of a screen.[56] And since the coronavirus pandemic, 49% of kids are now spending more than 6 hours a day online.[57]

As gaming and remote Zoom learning become the norm for many children and teens in modern times, the challenges to limit screen time increase, along with the factors impacting cognitive development. The issues seem to grow more complex for both parents and researchers! The organization, Children and Screens, articulates the current state well in a web post for an introduction to one of their webinars:

"Scientists are just beginning to understand the complex ways that digital media affect

On a typical day, children spend 4-6 hours and teens up to 9 hours in front of a screen.

brain structure and function in young people. Factors that must be considered include the unique vulnerabilities and characteristics of growing children, different patterns of use (e.g., multitasking, receptive vs. interactive use), diverse platforms, varied content and programming (e.g., educational programs vs. entertainment), as well as kids' exposure at different ages in differing amounts and contexts."[58]

Amidst all this complexity, I think it can help to define, what we mean by "thinking" and "cognitive function." If we define "thinking" as the ability to ponder a mental challenge over time, we would have to conclude that fast paced gaming and absorbing fast-paced images disrupt the slower thinking processes, necessary to grow abilities such as discernment, analysis and evaluation. With this definition we can consider educational programs, as well as slower-paced computer, app and video games, supportive of academic learning since they give kids time to think. In the case of video games, though, the outcomes are not as straight-forward. For instance, there are studies that indicate video game playing can support "cognitive enhancement" such as short-term working memory, but they have deleterious effects on selective and sustained attention—skills certainly necessary for "thinking" as described above.[59]

For a practical bottom-line we return to "patterns of research over time" to give us direction regarding media's impact on kids' critical thinking and academic performance:

In a 2019 large-scale meta-analysis of 5,599 studies from 23 countries published between 1958 and 2018 on the association between screen time and children's and teens' academic performance the authors concluded:

"Findings from this meta-analysis suggest that each screen-based activity should be analyzed individually for its association with academic performance, particularly television viewing and video game playing, which appeared to be the activities most negatively associated with academic outcomes. Education and public health professionals should consider supervision and reduction to improve the academic performance of children and adolescents exposed to these activities."[60]

In addition to this information, another large body of research can be helpful for parents who want to grow wise users of technology: Research patterns over time show unequivocally that media and digital literacy skills support critical thinking skills.[61]

My initial introduction to media literacy education was in 1992 at a Toronto Media Literacy Conference. The first workshop I attended opened my eyes. The professor showed us a beer commercial and then asked us what messages were being conveyed. We responded with our best guesses. Then we began "deconstructing it" frame by frame. Every 5-10 seconds the camera shifted focus and brought a new message for us to ponder. He asked us questions like, "Why do you think the light is behind the woman entering the bar and not around the men seated at the bar?" "Why do you think the camera rests on the can of beer longer than any other shot?" "Where is the focus of the men's attention?" "How is the woman dressed?" "Why is she dressed like that?" It took almost an hour to go through a 28-second commercial, but by the end of this thought-provoking exercise we were seeing connections between "sex sells beer" and understanding how camera angles and sound evoke special feelings to punctuate the message. Every single frame had an intentional purpose. As a former high school English teacher, I was hooked! "This is like analyzing a poem or a short story," I thought. And indeed, it was—the professor even referred to the images as "text."

A few years later, I wrote (with my colleague, Kathleen Bander): *Screen Smarts: A Family Guide to Media Literacy* (Houghton Mifflin, 1995), since I could see how media literacy education could be adapted in the home as parents talked to their kids about what they see on and do with screens.

In our current tech saturated society, we also need to add "digital literacy" to kids' understanding. While media literacy focuses on screen content messages, digital literacy considers why those messages exist in the first place. Dr. Jenny Radesky, pediatrician and researcher on children and media writes, "Digital literacy requires that children, teenagers, and parents understand that technology is created by other humans with their own agendas and that they can accept or reject its messages, identify advertising and persuasive intent, reflect on their own reactions to media, and engage with media on the basis of their own intentions (rather than reacting to engagement-promoting design)."[62]

To a large degree, children's and teens' thinking skills emerge from social experiences—especially with interactions with caring adults. True, most parents can't go frame-by-frame to analyze a commercial with their children or do an all-out research project on what companies own your teen's favorite video games. However, what moms and dads can do is to make discussions around screens and their purposes an integral part of daily family living. Doing this will not only grow children's thinking skills, but support their wise choices about how, when, and why to use any form of screen technology.

Dr. Radesky's research, as well as hundreds of other studies show, "Many digital media resources, including apps, programs, games, and educational materials, are subsidized and supported by advertising dollars. Children's and teenagers' unique developmental needs make them more vulnerable to negative physical, mental, and financial health effects of digital marketing. Although parents play a large role in helping their children be critical of media messages, identify surreptitious advertising approaches, and resist their influence, it is also crucial that there are measures in place in children's digital media environments to protect their needs."[63]

UNDERDEVELOPED IMAGINATION AND CREATIVITY

Developing a generative imagination in early childhood is critically important. Research conducted by Dr. Jerome and Dr. Dorothy Singer at Yale University for two decades showed the value of pretend play for growing children's imagination. They also found significant other benefits as well: "Children who engage in pretend play smile and laugh more, have longer attention spans and more satisfying peer relationships, and are less aggressive than children who do not know the joy of make-believe play."[64] Their research also showed that youngsters' creativity and problem-solving abilities decrease as their screen time increases. "Our data and observations indicated that heavy TV viewing did not seem to be conducive to the development of imaginative capacities. The heavy viewers seemed less likely to be our most imaginative children."[65] Other research has confirmed this. For instance, Valkenburg and van der Voort concluded after their a one-year investigation of several studies, "TV provides the viewer with ready-made visual images and thus does not provide viewers with practice in generating their own visual images."[66]

Joseph Chilton Pearce elegantly explains the impact of screen images on the young brain's imperative to make up its own images:

"Television floods the infant-child brain with images at the very time his or her brain is supposed to learn to make images from within. Story telling feeds into the infant-child a stimulus that brings about a response of image making that involves every aspect of our triune system. Television feeds both stimulus and response into the infant-child brain, as a single paired effect, and therein lies the danger. Television floods the brain with a counterfeit of the response the brain is supposed to learn to make to the stimuli of words and music. As a result, much structural coupling between mind and environment is eliminated; few metaphoric images develop; few higher cortical areas of the brain are called into play; few, if any, symbolic structures develop. $E=mc^2$ will be just marks on paper, for there will be no metaphoric ability to transfer those symbols to the neo-cortex for conceptualization, and subsequently, no development of its main

purpose: symbolic, conceptual systems."[67]
The risks involved not only pertain to infants and young children. **Patterns of research over time show that the imagination and creativity of older children and teens can be negativity impacted by excessive screen time—in three significant ways:**

1. Displacement of Time in Self-Generated Images
2. Reduction of Real-World Sensory Experiences
3. Distraction from Healthy Introspection

---

1. Displacement of Time in Self-Generated Images

A second-grade teacher told me this story: "I started reading aloud to the class after lunch on the first day of school, like I always do. All of the children were in rapt attention, with the exception of one little boy. I walked over to him and asked, 'What's the matter? Are you okay?' He was fidgeting and seemed agitated. He looked at me blankly and whispered anxiously, 'What am I supposed to do?' I replied, 'Well, I'd like you to listen to the story.' He seemed confused. So, I continued, 'We are quiet now and enjoying the story I'm reading.' He still didn't understand. We talked back and forth for a while until I got an inkling of what was going on for this child. I finally asked, 'Tommy, don't you see pictures in your head when I'm reading aloud?' He shook his head, 'No, should I?'"

With screen technologies every image is given. Absolutely zero images are generated by the child—so different from every image conjured up while reading. And, even if youngsters are browsing a picture book, there may be up to 40-50 illustrations. Yet, those pictures are only a part of the story; all the other story parts are constructed in the child's head. Contrast that with at least 2,000 images in a two-hour

movie, or thousands of images in a week of video game playing, and we can see that the cumulative result of a steady screen diet is under-exercised mental imagery.

Yet, image-making is critically important as it provides access to the symbolic functions of our brain, allowing us to imagine new possibilities—the first step in creating innovations. Studies reveal that when faced with extreme physical deprivation, imaginative people were able to discover new pathways out of their situations better than unimaginative people.[68] In his book, *Flow*, Mihaly Csikszentmihalyi describes the imagination as giving a person "a portable set of rules" in which to mitigate reality. "Whenever the outside world offers no mercy," he writes, "an internal symbolic system can become a salvation. Anyone in possession of portable rules for the mind has a great advantage."[69]

Making up one's own images in one's own head may have even more implications than previously thought. In his book, *A is for Ox: The Collapse of Literacy and the Rise of Violence in an Electronic Age*, Barry Sanders writes:

"The limbic system seems to feed on self-generated images. According to some researchers, when young people conjure their own scenes in the mind's eye, the heart produces a hormone that feeds the limbic system, strengthening it to generate more images of a more and more vivid nature. A strong limbic system provides a natural defense against the constant bombardment of images of sadism and violence that permeate contemporary consumer culture."[70]

Yet, we have been increasing screen time, while decreasing time in activities that require active generation of images. This trend alarms experts and researchers. For instance, from 2007 to the present many studies indicate concerns that "children's daily experiences appear to increasingly include screen-time experiences, which may come at the expense of time engaged in activities that require greater levels of mental imagery[71][72] such as reading[73] or imaginative play.[74]

Further alarmingly, time spent with interactive media does not enhance mental imagery capacities. A 2020 study of 266 children, ages 3-11, demonstrated that those using more screen media showed statistically significantly lower performances on mental imagery: "Mental imagery performance was lower in children exposed to more screen-time because they have less experience with the active creation of their own mental images." This held true for both passive media such as TV viewing and active media such as playing video or app games. The authors stated, "even…so-called active media types might still not involve much active imagery generation, especially in comparison to other typical childhood experiences (e.g., reading, imaginative play)."[75]

These patterns of research need our serious attention because there is so much at stake—for children, for families, indeed, for our society as a whole. Pearce, in *Evolution's End*, explains this well:

"Failing to develop imagery means…children who can't 'see' what the mathematical symbol or the semantic words mean, nor the chemical formulae, nor the concept of civilization as we know it. They can't comprehend the subtleties of our Constitution or Bill of Rights and are seriously…bored by abstractions of this sort. They can sense only what is immediately bombarding their physical system and are restless and ill-at-ease without such bombardment. Being sensory deprived they initiate stimulus through constant movement…unimaginative children are far more prone to violence than imaginative children, because they can't imagine an alternative when direct sensory information is threatening, insulting, unpleasant, or unrewarding. They lash out against unpleasantness in typical R-system [reptilian system] defensiveness, while the imaginative

These patterns of research need our serious attention because there is so much at stake— for children, for families, indeed, for our society as a whole.

child can imagine an alternative, that is, create images…that offer a way out…imagination gives resiliency, flexibility, endurance, and the capacity to forgo immediate reward on behalf of long-term strategies."[76]

2. Reduction of Real-World Sensory Experiences

Recent studies have shown that sensory and motor systems underlie mental imagery.[77] Indeed, various theoretical approaches have argued that sensory and sensorimotor experiences form the basis of mental imagery and cognition. With continual new understandings of the brain-body-mind connections, this makes sense—especially to parents who see the positive outcomes when their kids play and move on a regular basis!

It frightens me, in fact, when smart researchers equate touch-screen motions with real-world sensory activities. Touching a 2 D-screen is a very different experience for brain/mind/body than playing/feeling/smelling 3-D sand, for instance. The fact that I have to point this out to some cognitive scientists makes me wonder: "Are we now at Evolution's End?"

When kids are sedentary with screens, their ability for mental imagery is at risk. Researchers Suggate and Martzon sum it up well: "Studies show that mental processes and concepts are dependent on a rich array of sensorimotor information and processes."[78]

Healthy play, for instance, includes real-world experiences. In addition to what the child has seen on a screen, s/he may add characters from books someone has read to him or her, plot ideas from Grandfather's stories, and dialogue from something s/he overheard while on the playground. Instead of merely mimicking external television, movie, or video game or app game images, the child is using internally-generated images to create a personalized play experience.

Using various images from the real-world in their play is absolutely necessary for optimal development. The fact that many children only imitate what they see on screens for their pretend play is a cause for widespread alarm and significant intervention methods. Imitating only screen messages day in and day out, without role-playing other life experiences means that the screen images saturate his/her self-identity. They squeeze out other mental models of self. The child's choices begin to align with screen-generated mental pictures. For instance, it might become easier to kick and shove a peer because the inner mental model the child holds is one of kicking and shoving, having internalized those actions from violent cartoons

and video games. It is not surprising then that these behaviors become second-nature since the child's emotional range is limited to an aggressive, anti-social mental model.

Imitative Play	Generative Play
Behavior imitates external images	New behaviors emerge as child filters external images from lots of experiences and uniquely combines them
Replicates TV/movie/video game scripts	Invents own dialogue, makes up new words, employs poetic language
Only commercial toys	Empty boxes, kitchen utensils, junk mail, etc., whatever is available
Toys stay the same	Toys take on magical properties and become various things as child pretends
Uses memory to reproduce what is seen on screens	Uses images from screens, books, life experiences to weave an original, creative play experience

3. Distraction from Healthy Introspection

Remember as a child staring up at the clouds and daydreaming? Or leaning against a tree and thinking of nothing at all? These precious times in childhood and adolescence where nothing on the surface seems to happening are extremely important for building creativity muscles. Children and teens saturated by media images are missing the many gifts of "boredom." As social critic Walter Benjamin puts it, "Boredom is the dream bird that hatches the egg of experience." Yet, studies show that increased screen time negatively impacts day-dreaming and creative imagination.[79]

And, it probably won't surprise you that other studies have found that screen-time increases children's impulsivity.[80] [81] [82] This, of course, leads to less time spent in self-reflection, reducing the capacity for boredom. Yet, healthy introspection, going "inside oneself" is a vital human need. It supports staying open to new ideas during those frustrating down-times. It's necessary to hone imaginative and creative abilities. And it's a basic a requirement for understanding oneself.

Bottom line: Too much time with externalized images on screens prevents children and teens from knowing themselves. And, they can't value what they don't know.

A Word About Screens and Creativity

While excessive use of screens can stymie kids' imaginative facilities as noted above, their creative expression can be encouraged through using screens intentionally. Digital devices provide numerous opportunities for this. For instance, "Digital media allow information sharing across a variety of media formats, including text, photographs, video, and audio. Today's video games, for example, often represent a merging of both traditional and social media, as users can virtually "inhabit" impressively produced worlds and interact with other users in remote locations. Video game participants can even work collaboratively to co-create virtual worlds."[83]

Here we return to the many benefits of adult-guided, intentional use of digital devices to provide opportunities for kids' creative expression. A balance of creative activities without screens and with screens provides kids numerous ways to explore their talents and understand the gifts they have to offer to our world.

Matthew Fox, a respected theologian and writer, explains that "the etymological origin for the word 'hell' is helan, an old English word that means 'to conceal'...In other words, hell is our place of concealment. I believe it is our refusal to create...And if hell is concealment, then heaven must be creativity itself."[84]

DECREASED INTRINSIC MOTIVATION FOR SCHOOL LEARNING

Intrinsic Motivation can be defined as: The desire, will, or intention to engage in any activity for its own sake. Renowned psychologist Mihaly Csikszentmihalyi explains, "When experience is intrinsically rewarding, life is justified in the present, instead of being held hostage to a hypothetical future gain. To achieve autonomy, a person has to learn to provide rewards to him or herself."[85] In a screen-saturated society with continual reinforcement for tapping, swiping, and scrolling, many children and teens do not learn how to provide rewards for themselves. Consequently, learning, being its own reward, becomes difficult. This is especially true for school learning, which requires focus, concentration, mental effort, experimentation, problem-solving, and risk taking.

The impact of screen time on children's and teens' intrinsic motivation for learning and for developing a positive image of themselves as learners can best be framed within the context of the question: Where is the child's attention when s/he is watching television? George Comstock, a researcher on children and media, makes this important point: "Although television may not tell us what to think, it is very successful in telling us what to think about."[86]

When a teen is playing a violent video game, he is not putting attention, focus, and labor into school studies; when a four-year-old sits for two hours in front of a YouTube video, she is not exploring her natural world and actively experimenting with problem solving. Many children may know how to read, and even read well, but choose not to read. Children's early fascination with reading is disappearing faster than ever; instead of tuning out in junior high school, they often lose interest now as early as Grade 3. Linda Phillips, the director of the University of Alberta's Center for Research in Literacy in Alberta, Canada states, "We know that most children start school and they're very interested, they're happy and they want to read. After they're in school for a little while, that starts to wane."[87] Dr. Philips is working with parents in the local community because many think that screen technologies are negatively affecting children's desire to read. "It's the computers," said Bob Hinchcliffe, a Regina father of two, including a son in Grade 3 who was surpassing his teachers' reading expectations for his age group until he could download computer games. As a result, his reading interest and literacy proficiency slipped.[88]

Screen overuse can affect children's and teens' intrinsic motivation by:

Keeping their attention away from self-involvement, self-talk, self-initiation, and self-discovery.

Their attention is on the influencer personality on YouTube, the special effect in the video game, or other external sources of gratification rather than the child's own interests and abilities.

Focusing their attention on objects and things rather than values, ideals, and personal meaning.

A smartphone is a tool, so are computers, video games, etc. However, if you buy art supplies, you use these tools differently. You must rely on personal values, ideals, and meaning to create what you want. Why is it so easy to forget about personal meaning and purpose when using tech tools?

Reducing the amount of personal effort and ownership put forth during a learning task.

What child ever felt pride or ownership after watching a YouTube video unless she was being guided to create something? What parent posts the daily hours his child spent time on social media on the refrigerator as a source of pride in her daughter?

As noted above, a systematic review of 58 studies between 1958 and 2018, presented in the *Journal of the American Medical Association* in September 2019—showed that as time with TV and video games increased, academic performance suffered.[89] Motivation for the slower learning processes integral to school work could be a significant factor for this decline.

Reducing the amount of creativity and exploration put forth during a learning task.

Youngsters who do not learn to explore areas of interest based on inherent curiosity become elementary school age children who are not motivated for classroom learning.

Limiting opportunities for losing self to the learning or creative task at hand.

Recall a time when the hours just flew by. What were you doing? Chances are you were focused on something that gave you much satisfaction. You may have been creating something or spending time with a beloved friend. When we are internally motivated by our actions, we tend to lose ourselves in those actions. Time flies by because we are so caught up in what pleases us. This kind of self-abandonment to the creative process is lost to children who don't have opportunities to spend chunks of time in uninterrupted delight.

To the degree that screen technologies keep children and teens from developing an inner life, their intrinsic motivation for doing things sans screens will be impacted. Bruno Bettlelheim has written, "The biographies of creative people of the past are full of (childhood) accounts of long hours they spent sitting by a river . . . roaming through the woods. . . or dreaming their own dreams . . . developing an inner life . . . it's one of the most constructive things a growing child can do."[90]

The Brain Process with Fast-Paced and Unmediated 2-D Screen Images

SENSORY DEPRIVATION

OVER ACTIVATION OF LOW AND MID-BRAIN AREAS

- Hyper activation of the orienting response
- Constantly changing images
- Less self direction of the attention process
- More distractability and need for physical release

UNDER ACTIVATION OF CORTEX

- Fixated eye movement
- Reduction in active cortical processing
- Less self-talk, prediction, and active thinking
- Less metacognition and active construction of meaning

Unbalanced development of brain functions

Negative impact on learning literacy, motivation, behavior and self-identity

EXPLANATION

The cumulative effects of four to five hours daily of sitting in front of a continuous flow of screen images without adult mediation are far-reaching. Although the child is quiet and safe, brain functions are being conditioned in very specific ways that will have long-term effects on thinking, learning, literacy, motivation, behavior, and self-identity.

Let's see how all this works, one step at a time.

Since screens are 2-D reality, they will:

DEPRIVE child/teen of on-going, vitally needed 3-D sensory experiences in order to develop optimally. In addition, they **DISTORT** the sensory input highlighting visual and auditory at the great expense of kinesthesis, proprioceptive, and olfactory experiences. And they **DISTRACT** the screen user from awareness of sensory 3-D experiences—2-D "experiences" become the predominant focus of attention.

In effect, with screens, the sensory nervous system does not get enough "practice" integrating sensory experiences into brain-mind-body. This in turn, inhibits normal development of brain function, under-activating the cortex and over-activating low brain regions.

Under Activation of Cortex

Fixated Eye Movement and Reduction in Active Cortical Processing

Sitting long enough, mesmerized by screen images, does "zone a person out," since eye movement, such as the type of movement a person's eyes do when reading, drawing, or manipulating anything in the 3-D world, is absent. Instead, the eyes stay trained on a small screen, keeping the cortex constricted within an inactive mode. (It should be noted that when children talk about what they see with an adult or a peer, they would not stay fixated in this passive state. The use of language necessitates the use of the cerebral cortex.)

Less Self-Talk, Prediction, and Active Thinking While Watching

With anything children or teens do as they engage in the world, from homework to learning a musical instrument to playing with blocks when very young, their thinking processes are interactively engrossed in a dynamic dance in which there is continual exploration, experimentation, and engagement. The cortex actively poses and solves problems, predicts outcomes, uses trial and error reasoning, makes judgments, initiates actions based on past experiences and past knowledge, and continually modifies and adjusts through self-talk what needs to happen in each and every instance.

There is no problem to be solved as a child or a teen passively takes in screen images. The child does not initiate anything, all is done for him or her. There is no exploration or experimentation initiated by the child. And in the case of interactive media, choices to explore are determined by the game or app.

Less Metacognition and Active Construction of Meaning

The younger the child, the less likely s/he will be talking to self while absorbing screen images. With no interaction from adults, young brains easily slide into being mesmerized by the images, so on her own, the child won't ask herself questions. Metacognitive abilities do not mature until about age 12, so children younger than 12 are extremely vulnerable to becoming zoned out by long-term viewing since they do not have the literacy skills to question inside of themselves what they are seeing on the screen.

However, older children and teens who use screens to "relax" and just sit and stare are not using many of their already developed metacognitive capacities in this cortically constricted environment.

Over-Activation of Low and Mid Brain Areas

Hyper-Activation of Low-Brain Orienting Response

When screen images change quickly, abruptly, and constantly, they trigger the orienting response within the low and mid brain areas. Children's cartoons, commercials, addictive app games and violent content in video games and films notoriously use the quickly shifting images to provoke emotional arousal, keeping a lid on thinking functions. The orienting response is a survival mechanism of our old reptilian brain, which allows us to flee, fight, or freeze when encountering a threat or a perceived threat.

Less Self-Direction of Attention Process

In a real sense, the screen has actually captured the child's attention process. Contrast this externalized control of attention with the internal control required while participating in any self-directed activity. The child or teen, not a scriptwriter or editor, actually determines how long he or she will attend to individual tasks. When engaged in a self-directed activity, the decision to shift attention from one thing to another is done within the child or teen as a choice governed by needs as determined by the child or teen.

Time with screens does not require the child or teen to be in touch with his/her human needs—in fact, the opposite is mostly true. However, if kids are in touch with personal needs such as the need to learn something new, to discover a solution, or the very human need to create something, screen images would not take so much of their daily atten-tion. But the more they are conditioned to become unconscious spectators, the more children/teens hand over their attention process to the externalized images, (or the tech people who created them and decided on their pace of presentation) and the less in touch they become with their own personal needs to use and direct their own attention in fulfilling and meaningful personal activities.

More Distractibility and Need for Physical Movement

By hyper activating low and mid brain regions, along with under stimulating active cortical functioning during the process of passive TV and video, the child or teen becomes much more at risk for learning and behavior problems. Being deprived of physical activity in combination with mental stimulation puts the brain in a sensory deprivation mode. By over stimulating the senses of seeing and hearing and under stimulating the other senses, the nervous system is bound tight, taking in "assaults of energy" from the screen with little or no physical release. Think prisoners of war who undergo torture techniques such as a continuous random drip of water while they are in isolation. Or any of us with the bathroom facet leaking tiny drips that we hear as big annoyances as we try to sleep. That leak, when all else is quiet, drives us mad and there is no sleep until we get up and take care of it. And most likely rant a bit to release our frustration so we can relax enough to drift off.

Much the same happens with hours of screen time. Because our nervous systems are constantly under assault, the predictable human consequence is the need to physically release pent-up energy when finally away from the screen. This results in much physical activity, running around, often out of control, especially in young children whose nervous systems cannot withstand the constant perceptual chaos of the salient screen flickering and whose bodies are just not designed to sit for that long a period of time staring at 2-D, flat surfaces. So, we can observe in children/teens with the habit of too much screen time: increased distractibility; less capability for concentration, focus, and attention on activities requiring slower mental processes, along with more aggression, whining, impulsivity, hyperactivity, and uncooperative, often highly stubborn behaviors. Of course, dealing day-to-day with such a child or teen, so adrift from basic developmental needs, is enormously stressful for any parent—no matter how conscious or mindful. It is no wonder we see so many well-intended, but highly frustrated parents wave the white flag to the tech culture and give up trying to limit screen time because it is the "only way to keep him or her quiet and gain any peace in the house." Yes, that is true temporarily. But over time the child will have many more difficulties as the screen spiral downward disintegrates the child's/teens' brain/central nervous system capacity for self-regulation.

We can't short-circuit brain development without incurring damaging effects. The brain of the child or teen must be stimulated in certain ways that can only be achieved through active participation in the 3-D world, or else the brain becomes conditioned for a continual state of frustration with self, rather than developing in ways which condition a satisfaction within the self that comes from competence and mastery of inner capabilities and fully functioning cortical processes.

The Brain Process in a 3-D Self-Directed Activity

SENSORY INTEGRATION

↓

Promotes normal development of brain functions

Stimulates development of Cortical functions

Reserves reactive functions of Low and Mid brain for real environmental threats

Developmental balance shifts toward dominance of reflective purposeful functions of cortex

The antagonistic aspect of cortical and Low/Mid brain functions are minimized

Coherent integration of overall brain system is promoted

Emerging personality grows out of a state of discovery, celebration and experienced competency in using full cognitive capacity

EXPLANATION

In 3-D reality, the brain and sensory nervous system work in sync, promoting a "fertile field" for optimal development. As an active, engaged participant in his or her environment, the child's/teen's brain/mind/body is also fully engaged.

In addition, the active cortical processes necessary in self-directed activities develop higher level thinking skills, metacognitive abilities, and allow for selective attention to mature. Since the cortex is in control of the self-directed mental activity, the low and mid brain areas are not hyperactive. In fact, the hyped-up mode does not exist (unless there is a threat in the environment such as parents' fighting while child is trying to do homework) since there is no perceived threat or assault to react to and no sensory deprivation to contend with. Rather, all brain functions can work smoothly, in harmony with each other, developing important integrative functions necessary for thinking, learning, literacy, motivation, appropriate self-controlling behaviors, and a self-identity as a capable learner.

It can be noted here that one important definition of a student, as defined in Webster's dictionary, is: "One who studies: an attentive and systematic observer." In order for our children and teens to be critical thinkers and successful self-motivated learners, they must be "attentive and systematic observers," spending much more time in self-directed activities which require their full participation in the 3-D world, while learning to use the 2-D world intentionally for their specific purposes, with their optimal development always the end in mind.

CHAPTER 2

Impact on Feelings and Behavior

INCREASED HYPERACTIVITY AND IMPULSIVITY

Screen time, as I discussed above, limits sensory input from the 3-D world, making focused attention, slow thinking and higher-level critical thinking more difficult than they need to be. Sensory deprivation also "revs up" the nervous system, contributing to hyperactivity and impulsivity.

Imagine that you are tied up and cannot move. Someone taps you gently on the shoulder. Then the person repeats the tap at regular intervals and keeps tapping for four or more hours! What would you feel like doing? When I demonstrate this imagined tied-up state in workshop settings, invariably kind, gentle non-violent adults give me such responses as, "Hitting you." "Lashing out." and "Screaming 'stop' at the top of my lungs!" They might do something they normally wouldn't think of doing in this imposed state of needing to discharge the pent-up energy that has been suppressed. As mentioned above, a leaky faucet could do something similar to us—especially at night. The drips magnify when other senses

are suppressed in the quiet darkness. There are good reasons why water torture works. Human nervous systems are extremely vulnerable to sensory deprivation.

Heightening one or two senses, while diminishing the others, will naturally put our nervous systems in a state of heightened anxiety, seeking urgent release. If the release doesn't come, the anxiety increases. Fast-paced screen content, violent video games, or app games that trigger immediate reactions, act like the tap on the shoulder while tied up or the sound of the drip while trying to sleep.

With typical screen entertainment content, images change approximately every 3-5 seconds or so. The youngsters' central nervous system takes the "hit." Again and again, for hours at a time. Consequently, vulnerable, developing nervous systems increasingly rev up. Now the child is wound up like a tight corkscrew. When the child finally gets away from the screen (usually with a fight or a battle), s/he must release all that pent up energy. Increased hyperactivity or "discipline problems" occur as the natural consequence. The child can't settle down easily, making the transition from screen

39

time back to 3-D life a nightmare for many parents. He's not trying to be difficult. She's not creating a fuss to make your life stressful. Physically revved up kids are actually doing what their brain/mind/bodies must do after screen time in order to regain equilibrium again.

Human nervous systems, especially young ones, require movement to disperse all that pent-up energy because of the sensory deprivation experienced being so long in 2-D reality. That's how human systems work. As the saying goes, "You can't fool Mother Nature."

Jerry Mander explained sensory deprivation well in his 1978 book, *Four Arguments for the Elimination of Television*.[1] In fact, sensory deprivation was one of his four arguments! Since that time, numerous studies have associated screen time with increased hyperactivity, impulsivity, restlessness, and difficulty concentrating.[2] And, the more fast-paced and violent the content, the more this effect is seen.[3]

Human nervous systems, especially young ones, require movement to disperse all that pent-up energy because of the sensory deprivation experienced being so long in 2-D reality. That's how human systems work. As the saying goes, "You can't fool Mother Nature."

One significant study was a 2019 Canadian study of 2,400 families. Preschoolers who spent two hours or more of screen time per day exhibited "clinically significant behavioral problems." Compared with children who had less than 30 minutes per day of screen time, these youngsters were five times more likely to exhibit clinically significant "externalizing" be-havioral problems such as inattention, acting out, hyperactivity and being oppositional; and over seven times more likely to meet the criteria for attention deficit hyperactivity disorder.[4] Piush Mandhane, an Associate Professor of Pediatrics in the University of Alberta's Faculty of Medicine & Dentistry who led the study, noted: "We found that screen time had a significant impact at five years of age. Current Canadian guidelines call for no more than two hours of screen time a day at that age. But our research suggests that less screen time is even better."[5] This would include educational

content as well. Given that there is a dizzying array of options available—for instance, over 80,000 applications tagged as "educational" on the Apple app store alone[6]—parents are often misguided into thinking, "At least the game she's playing is educational." Yet, in reality, the time being in a 2-D reality is the significant factor impacting the behavior in young children, regardless of the content.

Other studies support these outcomes. Dr. Dimitri Christakis, Director of the Center for Child Health, Behavior and Development at Seattle's Children Research Institute (whose research was mentioned in Chapter 1) found in a 2021 study that formal features of touch-screen apps can induce compulsive use in toddlers, leading to increased hyperactivity.[7] While another large Canadian study (2021)—this one with 1,992 families—found that youngsters predisposed to high-intensity plea-sure seeking and impulsivity, are more prone to use screens for entertainment, leading to increased behavior problems. The findings of this significant study suggest "that an under-standing of social risks and individual char-acteristics of the child should be considered when promoting healthy digital habits." [8]

Interestingly, lack of impulse control has been associated with teens and young adults not being able to put down their smart phones. Research over the past decade has shown that engaging with electronic devices during development (e.g., smartphones) stimulates powerful behavioral and neurobiological reinforcement. Since immediate response to maintain communication or gaming is re-quired the low-brain is constantly reacting quickly. This, in turn, promotes greater use of the device or the game, resulting in impaired inhibitory control, perseverance, emotion regulation, and weak impulse control—all conditions associated with heavy engagement with mobile devices! A vicious feedback loop, indeed. For instance, a 2016 study of male and female undergraduates, led the researchers to conclude: "The present evidence leads us to the conclusion that mobile technology habits, such as frequent checking, are driven most strongly by uncontrolled impulses and not by the desire to pursue rewards."[9]

Research has shown that engaging with electronic devices during development stimulates powerful behavioral and neurobiological reinforcement.

STIMULUS ADDICTION

Excessive exposure to fast-paced, and/or violent screen content can condition brains to actually come to need hyper-stimulation in order to feel satisfied, putting kids at risk for becoming addicted to hyper stimulation, both on screen and off.

Video game addiction, or "Internet Gaming Disorder" (IGD), has been included in the Diagnostic and Statistical Manual of Mental Disorders, 5th Edition, the reference manual U.S. psychologists and psychiatrists use for the diagnosis and treatment of clients.[10] So gaming addiction now falls into the category of a real addiction such as a drug addiction. Reinforcing techniques, like rewards for gaining new skills and beating opponents, are intentional designs to keep players com-ing back for more. Trying to beat the high score and continually "leveling up" naturally draws players in. Human brains love chal-lenge and actually enjoy the right amount of complexity. Video games deliver both novelty and challenge in a paced way that arouses and sustains interest. And, no matter how advanced a player becomes, there is no end. Continually, there are promotions for the next level or the next version of the game.

Although there are educational video games and plenty of ways gaming can be used for teaching and training purposes in healthy ways, the major concern comes with violent or fast-paced content that provides hyped feelings of excitement—the player actually becomes addicted to the stimulus created by the content. In the case of violent media, the child or teen can begin equating harming others with "pleasure."

Like any other addiction, stimulus addic-tion can only escalate. The child, as he or she grows older, needs more and more levels of violence—more graphic and horrific images—in order to feel the "high" and pseudo-satisfaction generated by the emotionally-laden violent image.

In an article, entitled, "Brain Research and Mediated Experience," Paul Gathercoal (a former State Media Studies Project officer with the South Australian Education Department) explains how media violence and fast-paced screen content, may become addictive. He draws upon brain research on the chemical-neurological connection and makes these important points:

- The difference between drug addiction and stimulus addiction is that with stimulus addiction the drugs (endorphins) are already inside the body; they simply need to be released.

- These endorphins are released in response to stress and to emotional experiences.

- An optimum level of endorphin release is maintained through everyday social interaction with the environment and its people, its challenges, its beauty, and the success and stresses of life.

- Children today grow up in a media environment that over stimulates.

- Children can come to biologically need a daily "fix" of violent content and build up immunity to manufactured horror. They then become incapable of producing socially acceptable emotional responses to real-life violence or human suffering.[11]

Anna Lembke, M.D., a psychiatrist and author of *Dopamine Nation: Finding Balance in the Age of Indulgence*, writes in a *Wall Street Journal* essay, "Digital Addictions are Drowning Us in Dopamine:"

"Twenty years ago, the first thing I would have done for a depressed patient was prescribe an antidepressant. Today I recommended something altogether different: a dopamine fast. I suggest abstaining from all screens, including videogames, for one month…Over the course of my career as a psychiatrist, I have seen more and more patients who suffer from depression and anxiety, including otherwise healthy young people with loving families, elite education and relative wealth. Their problem isn't trauma, social dislocation or poverty. It's too much dopamine."[12]

It's important to consider: When children and youth are with screens, they are not solving and negotiating conflicts with their peers in real life. Consequently, they are missing priceless opportunities to gain needed cooperative learning and social skills. And as the real world of slowness and struggle, decisions and demands becomes less appealing, children's psychological and physiological systems become more affected, leading to increased needs for stimulus addiction.[13]

Dr. Donald Shiffrin, a concerned pediatrician in the Seattle area, puts the effects of stimulus addiction in perspective, offering a radical alternative to daily video game playing:

"A definite drug response. When kids get into video games the object is excitement, mimicking drug-seeking behavior. Initially there's experimentation, behavior to seek the drug for increasing levels of excitement. And then there's habituation, when more and more of the drug is actually necessary for these feelings of excitement. Limit video game playing to one day a week. Everyone goes to Disneyland for a day. No one goes there daily."[14]

"Limit video game playing to one day a week. Everyone goes to Disneyland for a day. No one goes there daily."

INCREASED AGGRESSION, FEAR, INSENSITIVITY, AND APPETITE FOR VIOLENCE

It would not be hyperbole to say that thousands of research studies over the last 6 decades have identified four basic deleterious effects of screen violence, affecting children's and teens' feelings and behaviors.[15]

Before I provide research supporting each of these effects, I think it is important to distinguish between harmful, **sensational media violence** with its intent to glorify violent acts like murder and rape, and **thoughtful media violence** that shows the reality of the suffering caused by the violence. A documentary about the Holocaust, for instance, may show graphic violence, yet its intent is to inform and evoke empathy. We can think of this type of screen violence as "sensitive portrayals."

Sensational Portrayals of Violence

Violence is "an act to intentionally harm another human or animal." Its outcome is injury—physical or psychological, fatal or nonfatal. While violence is part of our world, sane parents don't seek out violence as a way to amuse their children. No one I know invites someone into their living room to brutally beat a dog, or rape another person for their kids to witness as "fun." Sensational screen portrayals of violence give children and teens a justification for violent acts, arousing pleasure centers in their brains, while skewing their understanding of the heart-breaking consequences of violent acts.

Portrayals of violence in the media that glamorize and/or sensationalize and/or sanction violence provide a socially aberrant environment in which it is difficult to raise emotionally healthy children. They can perpetuate socially dangerous attitudes, behaviors, and values, as well. In fact, the sadistic and psychopathic violence found in many popular video games pushes the boundaries of cultural norms into the realm of social deviancy.

Sensitive Portrayals of Violence

Sensitive portrayals of violence, on the other hand, can promote empathy and compassion because they depict real-life suffering and its consequences. Such portrayals can evoke understanding of the human condition because in no way do they suggest that the suffering caused by the murder or rape, for example, is "fun."

Four Major Affects of Sensational Portrayals

A steady diet of sensational portrayals of screen violence can result in one or more of these four negative impacts:

- Increased aggression and hostility
- Increased fear
- Increased callousness and insensitivity
- Increased appetitite for violence

1. Increased aggression and hostility

The possibility that screen violence increases aggression had been raised at the advent of TV. The first U.S. congressional hearings on the question took place in 1952, when only a quarter of America households had "television sets" and screen content was, by current standards, fairly slow and boring.[16] By 2000, based on decades of conclusive evidence, six prestigious organizations that focus on public health, including the American Psychological Association and the American Academy of Pediatrics, issued a joint statement that, in part, reads, "At this time, well over 1,000 studies… point overwhelmingly to a causal connection between sensational media violence and aggressive behavior…"[17]

Yes, doctors, psychologists, and psychiatrists really did say the word, "causal." Dr. Michael Rich, director of the Center on Media and Children's Health at the Children's Hospital of Boston, testified to Congress in 2003 that the correlation between violent media and aggressive behavior "is stronger than that of calcium intake and bone mass, lead ingestion and lower IQ, condom non-use and sexually acquired HIV, and…tobacco smoke and lung cancer—all associations that clinicians accept as fact, and on which preventive medicine is based without question."[18] Other experts have used the comparison of the link between a high fat diet and heart disease, as well.[19]

Consistently, large meta-studies analyzing hundreds of studies from around the world with various diverse populations, show that violent screen content, especially violent video games, increase aggressive thoughts, angry feelings, physiological arousal, and aggressive behavior and decrease empathic feelings and helping behaviors.[20]

Without adult mediation, most children and teens exposed regularly to media violence are

"At this time, well over 1,000 studies…point overwhelmingly to a causal connection between sensational media violence and aggressive behavior…"

at some risk. Research shows that they will be more likely to exhibit a hostile attitude, be more reactionary and defensive in social interactions, more likely to resolve conflicts with physical force, entertain more aggressive thoughts and be more likely to use bullying behaviors with peers.

2. Increased fear

George Gerbner, a distinguished researcher studied the effects of media violence on both children and adults over a thirty-year time span. His significant body of research consistently showed that a steady diet of violent screen content caused both children and adults to see the world and other people as more dangerous than they really are. He called this effect, "the mean world syndrome." Fear of others and fear of being harmed increased as screen violence increased.[21]

Once again, the pattern of young children being more significantly affected arises. For instance, children, even up through the ages of ten or eleven, won't usually say to themselves as they watch a frightening film, "Oh, that's great make-up, since the monster looks so scary." Or "The darkness on the set really makes the scene feel creepy."

No, they react to the visual images as if they were real, with their emotions engaged intently—not their minds. Youngsters are neither mentally, nor emotionally, equipped to be able to handle violent imagery. Consequently, what makes the strongest emotional impact on them is what they remember most readily.

In an interesting study, 90 percent of college students remembered being intensely scared as a child by something in the media.[22]

Night terrors, over concern for self-protection, fear of being alone, and untrusting behaviors are symptoms associated with children who encounter too much sensational, frightening screen violence.[23]

3. Increased callousness and insensitivity

Continuous exposure to manufactured horror can condition kids to become less empathetic to real-life suffering, less caring to those who are hurting, and less capable of responding appropriately to those in need. This desensitization effect of sensational screen violence can be thought of as "a virtual bystander effect." As in the real-life bystander effect, both diffusion of responsibility and social influence contribute to decreasing prosocial ways to help victims of real-life violence.[24] Research also shows that media violence increases tolerance of others inflicting harm, as well as becoming more tolerant of ourselves as perpetrators of violence.[25]

Researcher Jeanne Funk has linked the desensitization effect with increased aggression in her longitudinal studies on the subject. She writes, "Occurring as an unconscious process over time, desensitization to violence can be defined as the reduction or eradication of cognitive and emotional and behavioral responses to a violent stimulus. This desensitization prevents the initiation of moral reasoning processes that normally inhibit aggression."[26]

4. Increased appetite for violence

Hundreds of studies document this effect.[27] The more violence that is watched, the more the child or teen wants to see violence. Often, the violence must become more graphic and gorier in order to capture the child's attention. Violent entertainment can soon become "boring" if the violence doesn't escalate. Seeking

more violence in real-life is also an unfortunate consequence. Researcher Dr. Craig Anderson states, "High levels of violent video game exposure have been linked to delinquency, fighting at school and during free play periods, and violent criminal behavior."[28] However, if a habit of TV violence is started before age eight, children are more likely to become aggressive in later childhood and/or adulthood.[29]

UNDERDEVELOPED OR DELAYED SOCIAL SKILLS

Research patterns over time demonstrate two key components impacting children's and teens' social development in modern times:

- Spending more time on screens than in direct 3-D interactions with peers.
- Less 3-D family communication and activities

Less Real-World Interactions

Too much screen time keeps children and teens isolated from real-world experiences with peers. Less opportunities for these rich, personal interactions, means less opportunities for learning the "rule systems" of social order. Isolation can lead to depression, and in the extreme, to criminal behavior. Researcher Dr. Brandon Centerwall found that the most significant factor of commonality among men who have committed violent crimes is that they had watched seven hours or more of television daily as children.[30]

Much of kids' socialization today consists of communicating through smartphones and social media, making it easier not to acquire the traditional face-to-face social skills we thought necessary for developing relationships. 95% of teens now report they have a smartphone or access to one. These mobile connections are in turn fueling more-persistent online activities. For instance, 45% of teens now say they are online on a near-constant basis.[31] There is no longer time or space to connect non-virtually!

> **You need two doors in our tent. One for going in and one for the alligators."[36]**
>
> **- Ana (age 9)**

These drastic transformations of socialization radically alter standards for human interacting and expectations of what is normal for optimal development of social skills for children and teens.

For instance, research demonstrates that pre-teens today are not as adept at face-to-face social cues as their counterparts 10 years ago. UCLA scientists found that sixth-graders who went five days without even glancing at a smartphone, television or other digital screen did substantially better at reading human emotions than sixth-graders from the same school who continued to spend hours each day looking at their electronic devices.[32]

"Many people are looking at the benefits of digital media in education, and not many are looking at the costs," said Patricia Greenfield, a distinguished professor of psychology in the UCLA College and senior author of the study. "Decreased sensitivity

to emotional cues — losing the ability to understand the emotions of other people — is one of the costs. The displacement of in-person social interaction by screen interaction seems to be reducing social skills."[33]

One significant implication comes from a body of research by Barbara Frederickson. She has shown that positive emotions forecast broadened cognition, namely, holistic processing and attentional flexibility. "Smiling seeds an expansive mindset that may be a vital contributor to health and well-being over the long term."[34] When we express a genuine smile and feel authentically positive, we elicit a broadened cognitive state. However, a non-genuine smile won't support holistic brain processing. A component of a satisfying relationship with another person is the capacity to distinguish between genuine and non-genuine emotions by reading their facial features—a skill that requires practice through real-world interactions with others. Young children begin a trajectory of lessened social peer interaction when mobile devices replace play activities with peers. Research shows that in play scenarios children negotiate and learn social rules by experimenting and modeling adult behaviors. Too much time on screens, tragically, takes precious time away from playtime. As far back as 1975, cognitive psychologist Jerome Bruner reminded us, "We know now that play is serious business, indeed, the principle business of childhood. It is the vehicle of improvisation and combination, the first carrier of rule systems through which a world of cultural restraint replaces the operation of childish impulse."[35]

An additional challenge is that our screen-saturated society makes it difficult for children to mimic civilized rules of behavior. When media messages, rather than their own generative imagination (as discussed in Chapter 1), dominate children's play, how can they learn to think and to understand what is and what is not acceptable in the social order? For instance, in 1975 when children played, they included the adult models around them—the grocery store clerk, a bus driver, the librarian—because they had direct experiences with such adults. Imitating these adults in their creative play, they practiced and learned "social restraint," supporting their healthy social development. Today youngsters are at two disadvantages: 1) Many lack real-world experiences of interacting with a diverse range of adults to model expected social skills, and 2) Many youngsters are so absorbed in screen images with 3-4 hours a day on YouTube, for instance, they imitate only the children and adults they see on the screens—risking practicing anti-social behaviors in their play—unless caring adults intervene.

Less Family Interactions

Daily, family interactions and regular family activities are key for children and teens to learn healthy social skills. Actually, nothing can replace them. Yet, too often in these technological times, "family time" means: parents and children are together, each absorbed in their own digital device. Researcher and writer Shery Turkle has referred to this new way of being with each other as *Alone Together* in her book with the same name.[37]

As one parent put it: "It's so easy, just put your feet up … plug it in and it's over with … and he's watching a DVD and I'm on my phone … it's quiet and peaceful. It's like no conflict."[38] All parents can "get this." We need our regular downtime and tech can provide it for us on demand, anytime. Yet, when this "family time" becomes the norm, kids' social development is compromised. 2017 research by Kildare and Middlemiss reviewed 27 studies and compiled the three main take-aways:

- Children and teens mirror their parents' or caregivers' media use.

- Developmental and behavioral issues arise when media interferes with or decreases parent-child interactions. In other words,

if kids don't receive our positive attention, they will seek negative attention!

- Parents/caregivers who use mobile devices when with children and teens are less responsive—both verbally and non-verbally, to their children's bid for attention.[39]

Dr. David Arredondo, of the Stanford University School of Medicine and Public Policy Research Institute, points out that children and teens need other people, especially loving parents, to mirror back to them appropriate emotional reactions. He calls this "the reciprocity of connectedness."[40] A tangible reciprocal feedback loop is set up when humans interact. This type of reciprocity cannot exist with screens. Dr. Arredondo explains that reciprocal connectiveness alters frontal brain structure and enables the ability to read human feelings. It is a neurobiological process essential for family cohesiveness, and it is required for social integration.

Only in the presence of loving adults who are interacting with them can children develop the ability to initiate affectionate interactions and emotional availability.

"The biology of our species makes necessary a huge parental investment in order to achieve the fulfillment of each child's potential."

In addition, the future development of resiliency skills is largely determined by the quality of the parental bond. Animal experiments clearly show the protective power of security, and the brain damage that can occur when it is absent. The family relationship, the home environment, and other loving adult relationships work as protective factors for children and teens, increasing their ability to "bounce back" from adversity.

David A. Hamburg, President of the Carnegie Corporation of New York, succinctly gets to the heart of the matter: "The biology of our species makes necessary a huge parental investment in order to achieve the fulfillment of each child's potential."[41]

UNDERSTANDING OF PREJUDICE AND BIAS

Screens bombard children and teens with media messages that shape their attitudes, values, and behaviors. Too often, though, screen content in films, video games, and on social media contains prejudice, bias, and stereotypes. Left adrift without adult guidance these can come to pervade their thinking and negatively affect their social/emotional development. However, (as the patterns of research show) with parental conversations, meaningful dialogues with teachers, and growing high-level thinking skills, children can grow to spot and understand media depictions of prejudice and bias.[42]

We Return to the Impact of "Fast Thinking" When Taking in Screen Content…

It seems biased thinking can more easily come about with "fast thinking" rather than using slower reflective, thought processes. In a 2021 review article, Peter Nelson points out what is obvious—when we think about it! He argues that the need for a quick reaction for the user to respond to others on most social media, for instance, warrants a quick assessment that could lead to incorrect assumptions and dangerous judgments perpetuating paranoia and stereotyping people. He writes:

"Originally intended to be an aid to interpersonal connecting, it appears that social media platforms were designed without any clear understanding of how they would interact with the basic neural wiring of our alert-response cognitive central nervous system…My observations as a researcher and clinician have made me aware of how easily 'self-stories' take on a paranoid tone when the danger alert system is activated…Another element fundamental to the continuation of this course is the absence of direct emotional knowing that we usually experience in face-to-face interactions. With a lack of honest emotional and non-verbal signaling…the power of digital social media to amplify perceived danger signaling (from others' posts) …Fast thinking is an instantaneous projection (onto the other)… which is not generated from empirical data gathering and logical construction.[43]

Interestingly, kids who are caught up in following "influencers" or who become highly engaged fans of peer or adult screen role models are more likely to be judgmental of others than those who are not caught up in "fandom." Studies show that a preoccupation with influencers impacts kids' understandings of fantasy and reality.[44] And when they don't have a grasp on reality, kids are more apt to see the world and others in judgmental, often stereotypical ways.

The studies cited below, from a 2017 summary of the research entitled, *Social Group Stories in the Media and Child Development*,[45] punctuate the vital need of caring adults to talk with kids about what they see on the screen in order to form healthy attitudes about themselves and others:

- The American Psychological Association Task Force on the sexualization of girls reported that objectification and sexualization of girls and women is common in a variety of media genres and that exposure to this material is related to a host of negative outcomes in the areas of cognitive and physical functioning, body dissatisfaction and appearance anxiety, mental health (depression, self-esteem), and sexual well-being. Although many who work with adolescents are well aware of the range of problems that can result from identification with these types of images, it is important to understand that negative attitudes about body image and a desire to take (unhealthy) behavioral steps to conform to these ideals are seen in children as young as 5 years of age.

- Research found identification with Disney princesses and engagement with related products predicts female gender-stereotyped play that takes place 1 year later, even after controlling for previously existing gender-stereotyped play, in children 3 to 6.5 years. Similar associations exist with exposure to superhero and gendered advertising illustrating the profound impact of media in shaping children's toy preferences and the nature of their play at a period in which play is so instrumental to social and cognitive development and construction of gender and racial identities.

- Media portrayals can also influence positive qualities and associations. When teachers read fictional stories in which British children were friends with refugee children, for instance, prejudice was reduced compared with control children. In another set of studies, children and adolescents read passages from the Harry Potter series relating to prejudice or a control reading. Exposure to the Harry Potter series reduced prejudice toward immigrants, refugees, and homosexuals, compared with controls. Both these media reduced prejudice by modeling cross-group friendships and reducing anxiety about cross-group contact.

Spheres of Influence for a Child's Growth

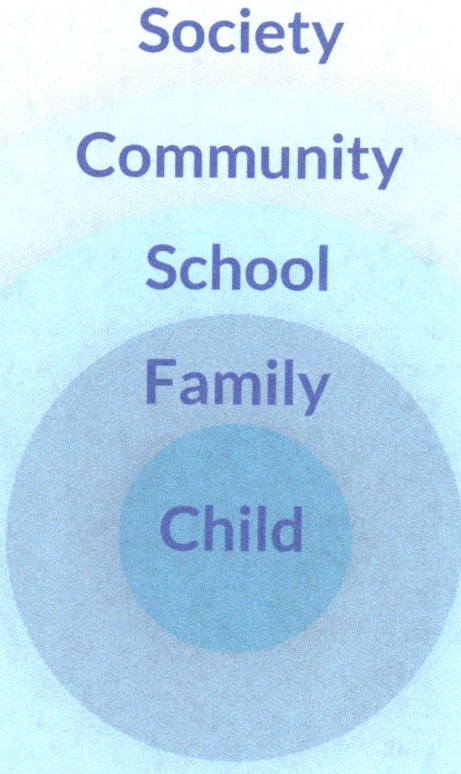

The child's sense of self-identity starts with the parent-child bond, and is held within the family. As the child grows, self-identity moves into larger, overlapping spheres of influence. From the relationsips and experiences encountered in these spheres of influence, the child absorbs and chooses experiences and images of (1) what is possible to include in his/her sense of identity, and (2) what is appropriate to include.

Spheres of Influence for a Child's Growth with Mass Media Influences

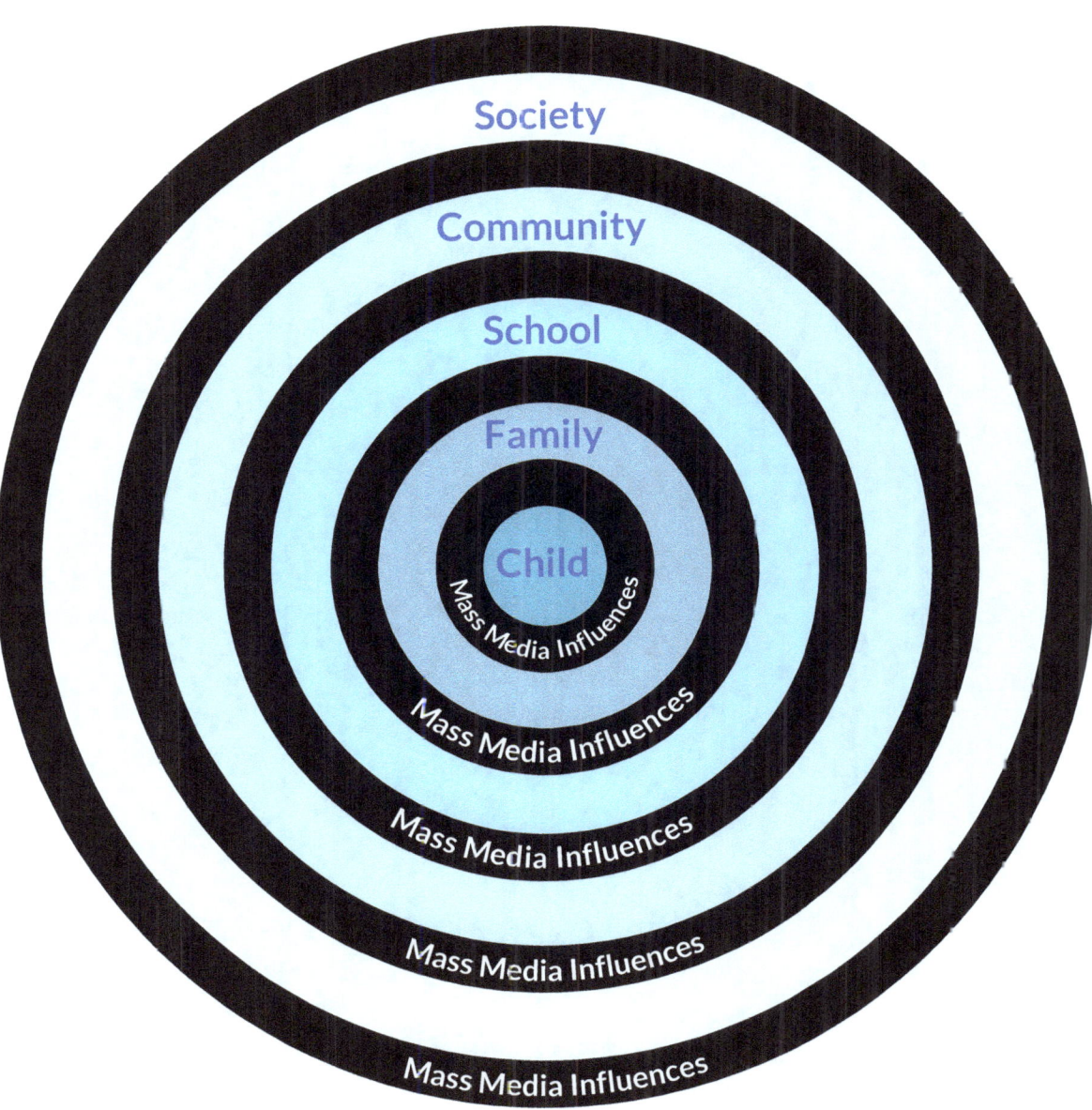

Mass media impacts the child within each sphere of influence. As the child grows, spheres of influence expand, making mass media effects pervasive and cumulative, because they are amplified through relationships in each sphere of influence. The earlier a child develops a personal relationship with mass media, the more we can expect mass medias messages to impact the child's self identity.

CHAPTER 3

Impact on General Health and Well-Being

OBESITY AND OTHER HEALTH CONCERNS

It is important to realize that well-researched studies on the relationship between screen time and physical health problems such as obesity, high blood pressure, and high cholesterol have been on-going for decades. Research conducted at Harvard first linked TV watching to obesity more than 30 years ago.[1] In 1991, the American Academy of Pediatrics issued a policy statement calling for the banning of television food ads aimed at children because they exploit vulnerable, young minds and contribute to obesity. "Television has been linked to the two most prevalent nutrition problems in U.S. children—obesity, which affects one in five youths, and high cholesterol levels, found in about a third of all children," said Dr. William Dietz, lead author of the statement and, at the time, an associate professor of pediatrics at Tufts University School of Medicine in Boston. He emphasized, "Not only do we believe that food ads should be eliminated, but also parents' control of the television set should be increased."[2] Although food ads aimed at children have been banned in some other

countries, like Denmark, for example, they continue to impact millions of U.S. children daily. A 2010 major study tracked the TV viewing habits and change in BMI of 1,100 young children over a five-year period. The result? The more hours per day of commercial TV that the children watched at the start of the study, the more likely they were to have a relative increase in BMI at the study's end.[3] Today, with targeted ads bombarding children and teens at every turn of the digital landscape, the negative impacts continue. According to Harvard's School of Public Health's website, "…food and beverage companies are becoming more sophisticated and targeted in their use of digital marketing and social media across these platforms, and public health advocates have called for stronger government regulation and industry self-regulation."[4] The untenable pattern, unfortunately, endures.

In fact, research studies that follow children over long periods of time have consistently found that the more TV children watch, the more likely they are to gain excess weight.[5][6][7] Other studies that followed children from birth found that TV viewing in childhood predicts

Thomas Robinson, a professor at Stanford University, has conducted a series of studies showing that too much TV, video, and computer time contributes, not only to obesity, but to aggression as well. Interestingly, in his studies, the content viewed didn't have as much an effect on aggression as the time spent being sedentary—something to note if kids are "acting out" after screen time. As discussed above in Chapter 2, being sedentary in front of screens doesn't allow for the necessary physical release of anxieties and frustrations caused by sensory deprivation. So, anger and aggressive behaviors are likely outcomes, in addition to obesity.[14]

obesity risk well into adulthood and mid-life.[8 9] Studies that include computer and smart phone use demonstrate similar trends. For instance, television viewing, along with computer use, obesity, and adiposity in U.S. preschool children were studied for the first time in 2007 and showed a relationship between computer use among preschool children and higher adiposity. This research also showed that a substantial percent (almost 36%) of U.S. preschool children exceeded the AAP recommendation to limit media time to two hours or less per day.[10]

Other studies with older children and teens have found that too much computer time displaces physical activities and contributes to the epidemic of childhood obesity in the U.S.[11] In 2019 two large scale studies, one in Finland, the other in the US, showed similar patterns. The Finnish study encompassed more than 10,000 children who were between the ages of 9 and 12. The results demonstrated that heavy screen time is associated with both overweight and abdominal obesity.[12] The U.S. study was a meta-analysis showing that increased screen time was a significant factor for increased obesity in children and adolescents.[13]

Lack of movement also has been shown to increase mental health symptoms, while less screen time coupled with more vigorous activity contributes to a lower risk of mental health symptoms.[15] A 2021 University of Washington study of 500 children ages 6-10 and 500 older children and teens, ages 11-17 during the COVID-19 pandemic revealed similar results. More physical activity and less screen time were associated with better mental health and less obesity, accounting for pandemic stressors. The authors concluded:

"Although there is notable concern regarding pandemic-related increases in weight gain and obesity rates, this study underscores that the same behaviors of screen time and physical inactivity are also associated with poorer mental health outcomes in children. Before the pandemic, three-quarters of school-aged children in the U.S. failed to meet physical activity guidelines; this situation has been exacerbated by pandemic-related circumstances and is particularly worse for middle and high school students. There is thus a critical need to reimagine multisector approaches to providing equitable opportunities for physical activity, including sports and outdoor recreation, for all children."[16]

We come once again to concerns expressed in Chapters 1 and 2 about the vital need for physical activity coupled with the reduction of screen time. Movement and exercise have been shown to improve cognition, including sustained attention, emotion regulation, and working memory, which are intricately associated with impulse control.[17] In fact, low levels of physical activity has been linked to impulsive behavior.[18] As children and teens sit in front of screens more time than they are up and about, they risk not only weight gain, and other physical health problems, but also they become more vulnerable to mental health distress, as well as learning and thinking difficulties.

"When considering the effects, the following must be taken into account with mobile phone use—duration, content, after-dark-use, media type and the number of devices—all are key components determining screen time effects."

Kids need consistent, daily physical activity. The Canadian 24-Hour Movement Guidelines for Children and Youth recommend that children ages 5 to 13 years accumulate a minimum of 60 minutes per day in moderate to vigorous physical activity, spend no more than 2 hours per day in recreational screen time, and obtain 9 to 11 hours of sleep per night. Their studies have shown that children who meet all three recommendations have better cognitive function, lower odds of obesity, better dietary patterns, and enhanced quality of life than children who do not meet any of the recommendations.[19]

More physical activity, along with healthy eating habits, reduce the risk of obesity and other health problems, like high blood pressure and diabetes. An interesting study suggests that families who eat dinner together with the television off eat more fruits and vegetables than those who eat separately or with the television on. To determine how family dinners and television viewing affect children's eating behaviors, researchers from the New York State Department of Health surveyed 1,336 participants in the state's Special Supplemental Nutrition Program for Women, Infants and Children. Study authors found that when families ate together, parents served more fruits and vegetables with dinner. However, parents served fewer fruits and vegetables when a television was on during the meal. Eating as a family or having the television on during dinner did not appear to affect the serving of milk. Researchers concluded that family dinners foster greater produce consumption and social interaction, noting that television viewing distracts both adults and children from how much they are eating. The findings support previous research suggesting that families that eat together have better eating habits, while young children who watch more television have worse diets. Noting that eating habits and preferences are established early in life, the study authors recommend that experts counsel parents "to promote family meal environments that support healthful eating."[20]

Extensive literature reviews show other physical health concerns associated with excessive screen time include high blood pressure,[21] low HDL cholesterol, poor stress regulation, insulin resistance, and reduced bone density.[22] A 2018 review regarding screen time and children's health made an important point: "When considering the effects, the following must be taken into account with mobile phone use—duration, content, after-dark-use, media type and the number of devices—all are key components determining screen time effects."[23]

LESS SLEEP AND MORE VISION PROBLEMS

Sleep

From babies to teens—most kids today are not getting enough sleep. And too much screen time plays a significant factor in this disturbing trend. In 2015 the National Sleep Foundation convened a panel of experts who developed the following guidelines for parents.[24]

	Age Range	Recommended Hours of Sleep
Newborn	0-3 months old	14-17 hours
Infant	4-11 months old	12-15 hours
Toddler	1-2 years old	11-14 hours
Preschool	3-5 years old	10-13 hours
School-age	6-13 years old	9-11 hours

A 2015 systematic review of 67 research studies from 1999 through 2014 found that screen time (e.g., television, computers, video games, and mobile devices) adversely affected sleep for school-aged children and adolescents. More than 3-4 hours daily and/or screen time right before bedtime shortened duration and delayed sleep in 90% of studies.[25] A 2017 Swedish study of 1,260 ten-year-olds found similar results, also demonstrating the relationship between insufficient sleep and obesity. They concluded, "School-age children who receive less sleep are more likely to be overweight and report excessive television and computer use.[26]

Screen time impacts young children as well. A 2017 study of 715 babies six months old to children age 3, found that every hour the youngsters spent using touchscreen devices, they lost 16 minutes of sleep. Using screens was also associated with sleeping more during the day and taking longer to fall asleep.[27]

"We can conclude: With the widespread use of portable electronic devices and the normalization of screen media devices in the bedroom, insufficient sleep has become commonplace, affecting 30% of toddlers, preschoolers, and school-age children and the majority of adolescents."[28]

It is well known that sleep deprivation affects the prefrontal cortex, striatum, and amygdala, contributing to hyperactivity and impulsivity and early sleep deprivation can result in long-term behavior issues.[29] And since research also shows that sleep problems in early life predict a greater likelihood of later development of psychopathology in childhood and adolescence,[30] an urgent need surely exists to highlight the importance of healthy sleep and screen time/media habits. A 2019 study puts it this way, "Impulsive behavior is associated with numerous mental health and addiction problems, including eating disorders, behavioral addictions, and substance abuse. This study shows the importance of especially paying attention to sleep and recreational screen time, and reinforces the Canadian 24-Hour Movement Guidelines for Children and Youth:

- 9-11 hours of sleep a night, and
- no more than 2 hours of recreational screen time a day

When kids follow these recommendations, they are more likely to make better decisions and act less rashly than those who do not meet the guidelines."[31]

Vision

A 2021 study of 201 myopic children, ages 7-12, showed changes in myopic progression during the COVID-19 home quarantine, associated with digital screen use for online learning, but not time spent on outdoor activities. Interestingly, children using television and projectors had significantly less myopic shift than those using tablets and mobile phones.[32]

"It has long been recognized that too much time spent on near vision tasks and a lack of time outdoors in childhood are the main drivers of the worsening global myopia crisis." *- Dr. Joshua Foreman*

Another 2021 study consisted of a comprehensive review and meta-analysis of over 3,000 scientific articles. The authors collected all of the research worldwide ever published on the link between smart device screen exposure and myopia. After analyzing and statistically combining the available studies, they revealed the most compelling evidence to date involving digital devices, in particular screen time, as a

risk factor for myopia in children. They found that the majority of these studies reported that exposure to digital screens (including longer periods of screen time and an earlier age of first screen exposure in children) was significantly associated at a higher risk of myopia, an increase in the severity of myopia and greater elongation of the eye which is the major anatomical change that results in the onset of myopia. When combined using statistical modeling, the results of all available studies have shown that, overall, high levels of screen time on a smart device are associated with a risk of myopia, almost 30% higher, and when excessive screen time, more than 4 hours daily, was added, it increased to almost 80%.[33]

Lead author of the study, Dr. Joshua Foreman of University of Melbourne hopes that the publication of these findings in one of the world's leading medical journals will be a call to action for more research into the effects of digital screens on the health of children's eyes. "It has long been recognized that too much time spent on near vision tasks and a lack of time outdoors in childhood are the main drivers of the worsening global myopia crisis. Mobile devices are a relatively new addition to our lives, and our research has highlighted emerging evidence implicating these devices as a key risk factor for myopia."[34]

LONELINESS, DEPRESSION, AND SUICIDE

The relationship of screen time to mental health issues has been a growing concern and interest of researchers in recent years. A 2018 study headed by Dr. Jean Twenge, scholar and author of *Igen: The 10 Trends Shaping Today's Young People and the Nation*, examined the relationship between screen time and depression and suicide rates in 506,820 adolescents in the U.S. between 2010 and 2015. The data on screen time use and mental health issues came from two nationally representative surveys of students in grades 8 through 12. Suicide rates were calculated from national statistics collected by the Centers for Disease Control and Prevention's Fatal Injury Reports. The analysis finds a "clear pattern linking screen activities with higher levels of depressive symptoms/suicide-related outcomes [suicidal ideation — that is, thinking about suicide — and attempts] and non-screen activities with lower levels." Among participants who used devices for over five hours each day, nearly half – 48% — reported at least one suicide-related outcome. In comparison, 29% of those who used devices for just an hour per day had at least one suicide-related outcome. Overall, during the time studied, suicide rates, depressive symptoms and suicide-related outcomes increased. Girls accounted for most of the rise – they were more likely to experience depressive symptoms and suicide-related outcomes than boys; they also experienced stronger effects of screen time on mental health. In particular, girls, but not boys, had a significant correlation between social media use and depressive symptoms.[35]

It should give us pause, that from 2010 to 2014, rates of hospital admission for self-harm doubled for girls, ages 10-14, while not increasing for boys and young women.[36] Writing in a 2021 *Atlantic Monthly* article, "The Dangerous Experiment on Teen Girls," social psychologist Jonathan Haidt points out:

"Facebook's own research leaked by the whistleblower Frances Haugen, shows: 'Teens blame Instagram for increases in the rate of anxiety and depression … This reaction was unprompted and consistent across all groups…' Researchers also noted that 'social comparison is worse' on Instagram than on rival apps. Snapchat's filters 'keep the focus on the face,' whereas Instagram 'focuses heavily on the body and lifestyle.' A recent experiment confirmed these observations: Young women were randomly assigned to use Instagram, or use Facebook…for seven minutes. The researchers found that 'those who used Instagram, but not Facebook, showed decreased body satisfaction, decreased positive affect, and increased negative affect.'"[37]

And vulnerable populations of both males and females, are also at risk. For instance, a 2021 study of digital media use of 192 children and adolescents, ages 8-16 with ADHD, during the COVID-19 pandemic, showed that those who already had a high level of digital use—defined as problematic—showed "significantly worse symptoms" with anxiety and depression than those kids who had limits on gaming and screen use.[38]

The data keeps piling up to demonstrate that excessive screen time is associated with depression, loneliness and suicidal thoughts. A major 2018 study found that "depressive symptoms and suicidal thoughts are associated to screen time induced poor sleep, digital device night use, and mobile phone dependency."[39] And a 2019 meta-analysis review of 7 cross sectional studies along with 12 longitudinal studies concluded, "Screen time based sedentary behavior is associated with a higher risk of depression, especially when it exceeds two hours a day. In the female population, the association between sedentary behavior and risk of depression is significant, while in the male population, no significant associations were observed. Our review supports the current recommendations of limiting screen time to promote mental health."[40]

Parents can support their children's and teen's mental well-being by reducing screen time and increasing their physical activity. Significant research, over an 11 year-period concluded that "more physical activity and less screen time are positively associated with mental health in adolescents and that interventions to reduce screen time may be beneficial for concurrent reductions in symptoms of depression and anxiety, irrespective of physical activity."[41]

DEVELOPMENTALLY INAPPROPRIATE SEXUAL ACTIVITY AND VULNERABILITY TO EXPLOITATION

Understanding the impact that viewing pornography has on children, pre-teens and teenagers increases in urgency with each new device and app available to younger and younger children. In addition to the early use of devices, other factors drawing adult attention and actions include "the high rates of sexual attack and abuse, the mainstreamed nature of pornography within society, the perceived vitality of media and technology in the lives of today's young people, the position that pornography holds as a sexual educator for young people, and the changed nature of the sexual lives of young people."[42]

The research summarized below focuses on research showing how engaging in pornography or sexual online activities, such as sexting, impacts sexual behaviors and attitudes and also increases kids' risk of exploitation by sexual predators.

Sexual Behavior and Attitudes

If you know an 11-year-old boy (maybe a son, a nephew, a neighbor, a student) chances are he's already seen hard-core pornography. Studies show that approximately 53% of 11-to-16-year-olds have seen online porn. Boys first view mainstream hardcore pornography at the average age of 12. Research has demonstrated that boys exposed to pornography from a young age are more likely to:

- believe "rape myths" that justify or defend rape
- have decreased empathy for rape victims
- display increasingly aggressive behavioral tendencies
- pressure their partners to engage in porn-style sexual activity
- experience difficulty in developing intimate relationships with partners
- have attitudes that support sexual harassment and violence against women
- develop sexual preoccupation and compulsive internet use [43]

Gail Dines, Ph.D., the nation's leading scholar and researcher on the effects of porn on kids and society, refers to pornography as the "the world's de-facto sex education system." She states, "It used to be that we could assume, with some accuracy, that when a teen boy rapes a young girl, the boy is acting out the abuse that he's endured. Today it is more complicated because he could be acting out scenes he has seen in pornography."[44]

A growing trend, which complicates the matter further, is that children as young as 9 years-old are engaging in sexually explicit screen activities. For instance, a 2021 report found that 1 in 7 children aged 9-12 years-old shared their own nude photos on their cell phones during 2020. This was almost triple the number from just one year earlier.[45] The report also found a sharp increase in the number of children – again aged 9-12 – who admitted that they'd seen non-consensually re-shared nudes of others. And tragically, they were more likely to think that sharing nudes is normal among kids their age.[46] When children become drawn into online sexual activities early on, and consider sharing nude photos of themselves and others as "normal," the leap into darker forms of sexual content as they grow older can be expected. It is sobering to realize that 88% of scenes in top rented and downloaded porn contain violence against women.[47]

"I'm angry about this as I know you are. And in a few years, these children will be angry, too....They are going to ask, 'Why didn't anyone intervene to protect me?'"

The road to seeking abusive sexualized content as entertainment and self-satisfaction must begin somewhere. It's important for parents and professionals to realize that popular media does little to discourage kids' early preoccupation with sexually explicit images. The Netflix film, "Cuties," for instance, received wide criticism for sexualizing 11-year-olds. It included a scene in the film where the lead character pulls down her pants, snaps a picture of her genital area and uploads it to social media. When Disney owned Hulu, a

program called "A Teacher," normalized sexual relationships between teachers and schoolchildren; and another show "PEN15," depicted an underage character masturbating in front of a mirror. AT&T/HBO's "Euphoria" depicts sexual relations between a teen and an adult, while Netflix's "Big Mouth" shows a 12- or 13-year-old boy offering to perform a sex act on his own father, as well as multiple scenes with full-frontal nudity of children in sexualized situations.[48] Is it any wonder that a third of young people have seen porn by age 12?[49]

The watchdog organization, Parents' Television and Media Council, puts the critical issues in clear focus:

"...why are we seeing such a dramatic increase in sexualized behavior by and among children? Because we are simultaneously seeing a dramatic increase in sexualized behavior on-screen, particularly in entertainment marketed to and consumed by children. The greatest blame lays squarely at the feet of those in the entertainment industry who have made a practice of sexualizing children, and who are normalizing the sexual exploitation of children. I'm angry about this, as I know you are. And in a few years, these children will be angry, too. In a few years, they are going to look back on their lost childhood. On their lost innocence. And they are going to ask: "Why didn't anyone intervene to protect me?" "Where were the adults when this was happening to me?" "Why was I denied my childhood?" [50]

Many studies over the past decade clearly demonstrate that the more time children and teens are involved with online sexual content and/or sexualized activities, the more their sexual behaviors and attitudes are impacted. A 2011 study demonstrated that mass media "exert a causal influence on United States youth sexual behavior." [51] A 2016 systematic review and meta-analysis showed a strong

association between self-reported exposure to sexual content on devices and in social media with sexual behaviors in teens.[52] A 2017 longitudinal study among 1,467 adolescents (aged 13–17, 50% male/50% female), found that exposure to sexually explicit Internet material directly predicted adolescents' willingness to engage in casual sex. In addition, exposure to sexy self-presentations of others on social network sites and sexually oriented reality TV predicted adolescents' willingness to engage in casual sex indirectly through descriptive peer norms on casual sex.[53]

A meta-analysis of 22 studies between 1978 and 2014 from seven different countries concluded that pornography is associated with an increased likelihood of committing acts of verbal or physical sexual aggression, regardless of age. The studies also showed an "overall significant positive association between pornography use and attitudes supporting violence against women."[54]

Viewing porn also affects the brain, shaping it for addiction. To date, at least 56 neurological studies support the premise that Internet porn use can cause addiction-related brain changes.[55] In light of the fragility of young brains ("What gets fired, gets wired."), I believe this significant research provides an added cause for alarm and activism on the part of all concerned adults.

"Never underestimate the power of the addiction", urges psychologist John Mark Haney. In the article, "Teenagers and Pornography Addiction: Treating the Silent Epidemic," sponsored by the American Counseling Association, he writes:

"With pornography, professionals sometimes fail to understand the power of the compulsion youth are facing, and it is not uncommon for school, religious, or private-sector professionals to advocate a simple treatment plan that is based upon willpower or moral character. Since pornography can be an addiction, these "just say no" types of approaches are likely to only create more frustration and self-defeating ideation in teenagers who do not have the willpower to stop. For such young people who can no longer control their actions, the intervention and treatment modality must recognize the problem as a full addiction, and treat it with the same consideration given to alcohol or chemical substances."[56]

Safety

Interacting with strangers online is an alarmingly regular occurrence among today's children and teens. A 2019 survey of almost 4,000 children found that 43 percent of those aged between 8 and 13 years old are talking to people they have never met in real life on social media and gaming platforms.[57] A 2021 follow-up study indicated that one third of 9–17-year-olds say they have looked for new friends or contacts online. 28% say they have had contact with someone online that they have not met before face-to-face. 12% of children state they have gone on to meet in-person contacts they had first made online.[58]

A 2021 study of 16,000 children, in grades 4 through 12, conducted by the West Australian Commissioner for Children and Young People revealed similar, and even more concerning results. About 17% of 7th-12th graders said they were in contact with strangers online at least once a day, as were 8.5 % of 4th through 6th graders. Almost half of all high school students reported "regularly" chatting with strangers online. And 56% of female students reported online sexual harassment in the form of unwanted pornographic messages and images, a figure that suggests such abuse is now "normal." Thirty percent of boys also said they'd been targeted for such material. Researchers concluded that for both genders, these figures represented a rise over previous surveys.[59]

Children are open prey for predators with many apps allowing anyone to contact them. Many parents don't know about this, nor do they know they can turn off the function that allows strangers to contact their children. Roblox, a game popular with eight-year-olds, is a good example of this seemingly innocent entryway into becoming sexually victimized. According to the organization Family Zone, "Roblox appeals directly to children under 12, who are easy targets who lack the ability to discriminate between appropriate and inappropriate requests. Roblox invites players to explore imaginary worlds of all kinds. Some of these are sexual in nature. One British dad who decided to check out the game his sons were obsessed with was shocked to discover avatars having virtual sex, ABC News reported in 2017."[60]

Roblox invites players to explore imaginary worlds of all kinds. Some of these are sexual in nature. One British dad who decided to check out the game his sons were obsessed with was shocked to discover avatars having virtual sex.

LESS PERSONAL AGENCY AND SELF-UNDERSTANDING

Conrad Kottak, an anthropologist who has conducted a five-year longitudinal study of TV viewing in Brazil and in the United States, found that the more TV watched as children, the more TV values shaped those children as adults.[61] And this makes sense when you think about it. Images can be powerful conveyors of priorities. They evoke strong emotions and often portray captivating content that taps desired longings. Images on 2-D screens stay with us. So, without adult mediation, screen content can influence children and teens since they are in the process of identity-formation—they can't be expected to have the necessary boundaries and self-understanding to resist inappropriate or potentially damaging content. In fact, without caring adults to help interpret screen content for them, kids are left lost in the tech landscape without a north star to guide their growing sense of personal autonomy, pro-active agency, and self-understanding. For instance, research clearly demonstrates that with more media use, children and teens are more self-critical—girls more often with body-image; boys with confidence in goal attainment.[62] What do they say about themselves as they are watching and talking about YouTube influencers, for instance? We can be fairly sure; most kids are not countering negative messages they receive about themselves with positive ones.

In a 2019 study of 127 10–13-year-olds, who regularly watched vloggers on YouTube, researchers found that for the majority of children their degree of bonding with the vlogger predicted the time spent viewing vlogs and that the vlogs were highly persuasive for the children recalling products and brands mentioned by the vlogger. How do vulnerable kids separate their own identity from that of the vlogger they so admire? How do they come into their own sense of personal agency and self-awareness? It is very difficult for them to do so without adult help "unpacking" the vlogger's messages. The researchers in this study made an important point: "Because of the popularity of online (social media) channels among youth, companies dedicate a significant proportion of their marketing budget on online influencer marketing. Therefore, it is important to acquire insight into children's processing of online persuasive messages."[63]

They cannot possibly grow a healthy sense of self, left to their own devices, so to speak.

And once again we see that the more vulnerable the child, the greater the impact. Sadly, it is not uncommon to hear that a child or a youth died imitating something they saw on social media. In a December, 2021, CBS news report, for instance, Instagram CEO Adam Mosseri, appeared before a Senate subcommittee investigating the social media platform's potentially harmful impact on young users. A 15-year-old who died as a result of a "Choking Challenge" on Instagram catalyzed the investigation. During the hearing it was pointed out that no one knows the "secret sauce" Instagram uses in its algorithms to portray specific content to specific individuals.[64] This unfair advantage is exacerbated when parents are also not involved. Yet, with Instagram and other platforms—that's the point—kids want to be out from their parent's surveillance as they grow into their own autonomy.

Yet, if digital experiences are their only way to do that, we can predict that the trend of increased mental illness among our youth to only continue. They cannot possibly grow a healthy sense of self left to their own devices— so to speak.

And quite hopefully, when parents are consistently involved, especially when they convey their values regarding media and technology, kids will take on those values, rather than the values of screen images, and are in turn, more likely to develop a healthy sense of self.

A national study of 465 pairs of school age children and their parents, for example, clearly demonstrated that parental attitudes toward the Internet predicted parent-child differences in perceptions of how frequently the child used the Internet for help with homework, and also predicted the child's healthy identity development. Bottom line: When parents used the Internet as a selective, intentional tool, so did their children.[65]

> **With a strong, healthy self-identity of themselves as learners and creators, children can grow up using all forms of screen technologies competently and age-appropriately.**

Impact of Media Images *Without* Adult Mediation

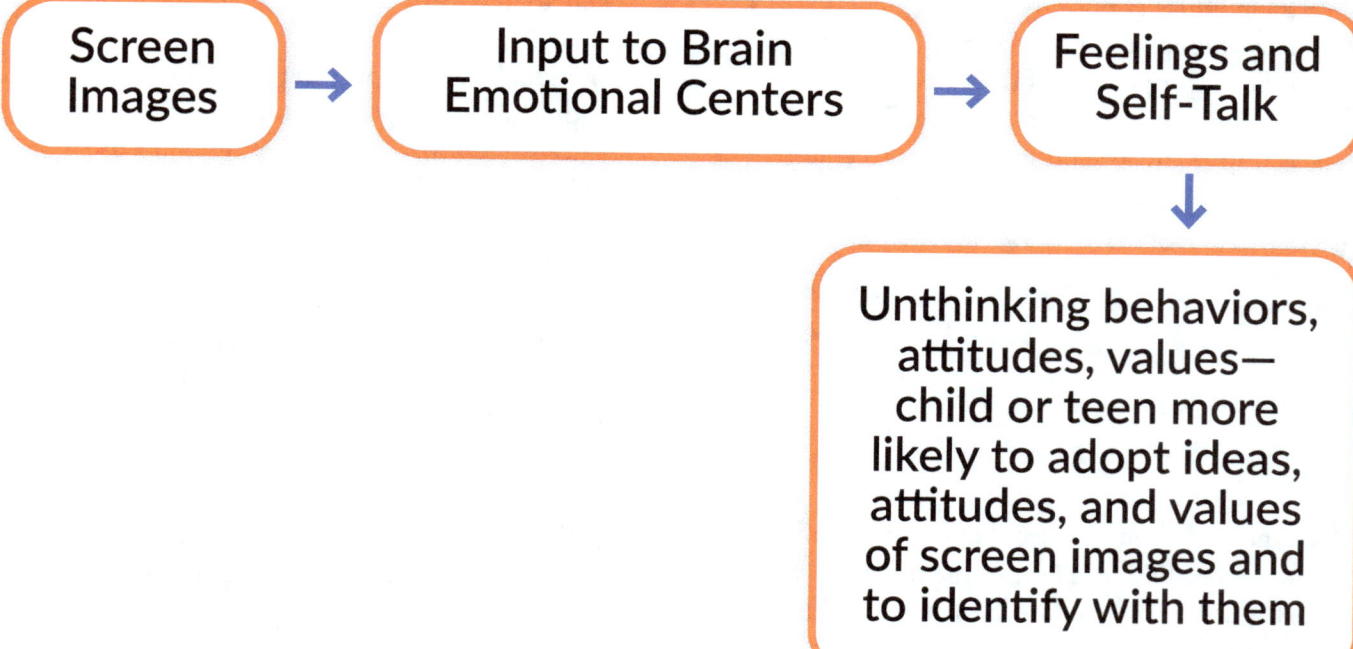

Explanation

In the above chart, we see that the screen images and/or content are being taken in by the child or teen without adult mediation. No other interpretation is given to the child or teen about the message Big Tech sends. The child or teen is completely vulnerable to the message. S/he may not be able to decipher important nuances that might make significant differences. Consequently, what the child or teen says to self about self and about the message are entirely up to the child or teen—with an immature brain and a budding sense of self.

Impact of Media Images
With Adult Mediation

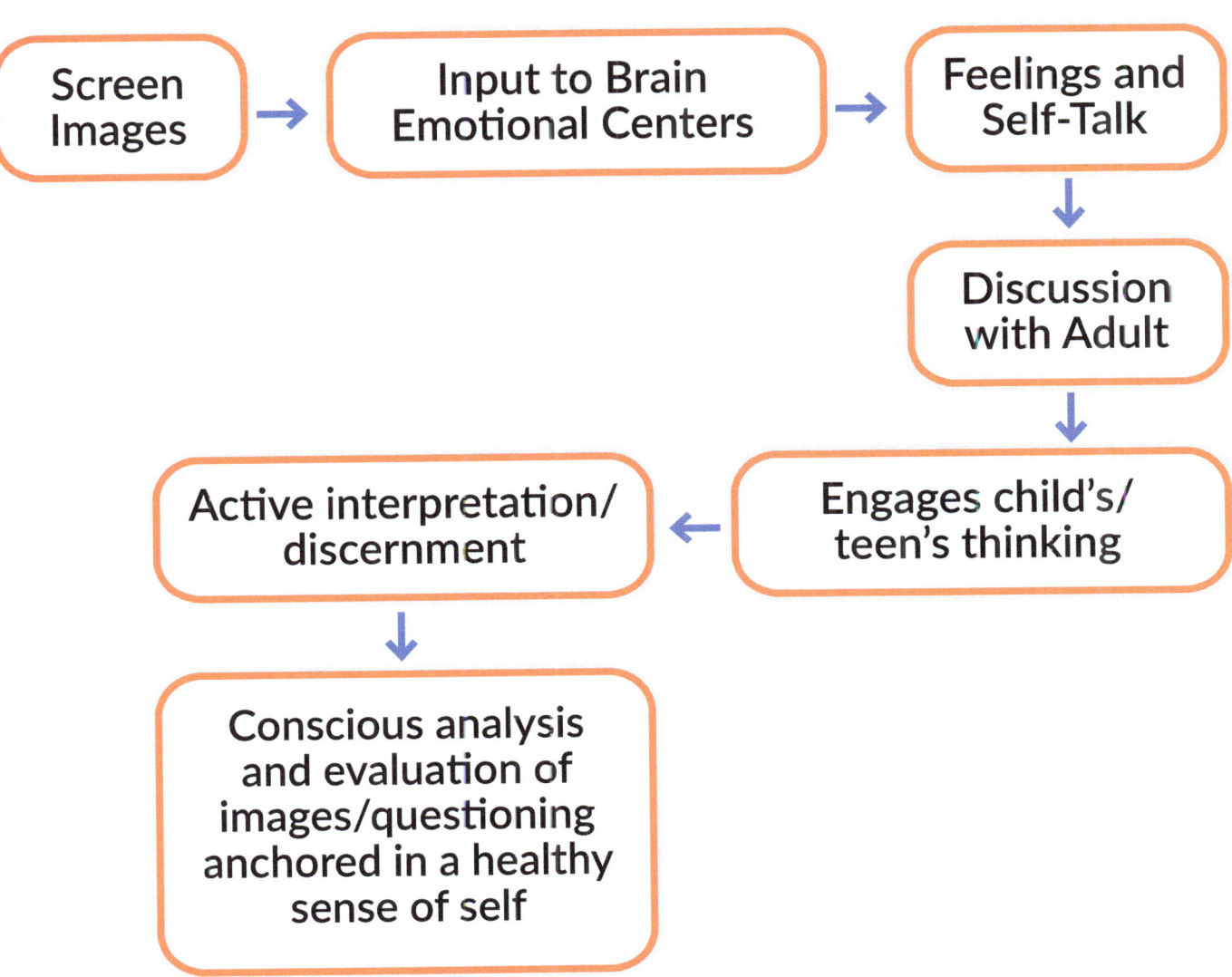

Explanation

In the above chart, the screen images and/or content are being taken in by the child or teen with adult mediation. Now there are opportunities for interpretation and discernment about the message Big Tech sends. The child or teen becomes more in control of how s/he responds to screen images or screen content. S/he may not be able to decipher important nuances that might make significant differences, but the adult can point these out and invite reflection and discussion. Consequently, what the child or teen says to self about self and about the message is more likely to be put in perspective. Even if the message is debated, the child's or teen's immature brain and a budding sense of self has been offered adult guidance and alternative ideas to consider. The adult has expressed values and priorities that will affect the child's or teen's developing self-identity over time.

A Final Word...

Creating New Patterns Over Time

If you have read this far, you now may be feeling completely overwhelmed, frustrated, sad, angry, infuriated. I understand. I feel one or more of these emotions regularly. The issues are daunting, no doubt about that. The patterns over time clearly point to a downward spiral, affecting children, families, and society as a whole on many levels. Yet, the research patterns also bring into focus how to make positive changes: **Reduce screen time and have kids do something else, instead.**

Yet, as we know that "simple solution" is mighty difficult to actually do. The parents I work with want to reduce their kids' screen time. They know it's better for healthy development. And usually, they even know what do. **Where most get tripped up is in the how.**

How to change kids' screen-time patterns in a world where they need to be on screens and they want to be on screens and besides, all their friends are on screens 8 hours a day and see, their parents let them, etc. etc. And all this at a time in their development when they are most susceptible to screen enticements to shape their brain irrevocably to want more and more screen time. Compounded complexity.

Yet, what is the alternative? What trajectory are we on as a society if we do not disrupt these past patterns and create new healthy patterns for our kids?

Screen and digital technologies, owned by a few who drive society to use them, are designed (whether intentionally or not) to keep parents at a disadvantage. Parental influence wans as tech influence intensifies, impacting structures and functions of young brains, minds and bodies in absolute ways. And, at the same time in the stew of modern-day stresses, parents remain preoccupied and distracted. So, of course, well-meaning parents find it difficult to know and focus on their children's growth imperatives. Tech keeps adults, and children alike, distanced from the core essentials that make and keep us human.

To help parents reduce their kids' screen time in the midst of all the challenges, I believe the first place to look is in our hearts and in the heart of every parent. Parental love is potent—powerful beyond measure. And the heart has help for us, if only we tap its vast resources.

I am continually inspired by the moving words of Brother Richard Rohr:

"Our heart…is the force that complements our other powers. It takes us beyond our limits. It contains our ability to reach out so it is the antidote to despair. We are spiritually coded in ways we have not yet dared even to imagine."[66]

As humans, and as spiritual beings, we have the capacity to disrupt this current, despairing unsustainable way of rearing children and teens. We can create healthy new patterns that support their optimal development.

And these new patterns can begin small. They will grow over time, positively affecting many aspects of a child's well-being. For instance, reducing screen time by 15 minutes a day, gives a child back 91 hours in a year…910 hours or 38 days over a decade…

to do something else! And in that doing something else, new possibilities naturally present themselves. Hues, nuances, and whispers, previously ignored can now be seen, observed, and heard. New discoveries abound. The real world formerly fogged over when looking through technology's lens, now comes into clear focus—the world's beauty now cherished, its slowness enjoyed by children who now actually see and directly experience it. And then magic happens.

It usually goes something like this…

The time she spends digging up mushrooms prompts her to say to herself, "I really like doing this. I think I'll ask my teacher if we can plant a garden this spring in the space by the playground." New ground has been broken in her mind, as well. What will it grow a decade from now?

The time he takes walking the dog has him noticing the animal's slight limp, which has him bringing it to an adult's attention, reflecting to himself, "I wonder what it would be like to be a vet?" A new possibility occurs to him. How will he understand himself as he ponders this potential vision of himself?

Yes, dear friends, life presents multitudes of opportunities for our children to grow healthy—strong in mind and body, vibrant in spirit, self-aware, creative and generative —attuning to their magnificent potential during their formative years. When we turn their attention back to life, our children and teens become enlivened. When this happens, they are more apt to control screens because they know they are the ones in control. And surely, rather than making technology their entire life, they will keep it in its rightful place—a tool to serve their rich and varied life.

References

Introduction

1. Lauricella A. R., et al. The common-sense census: plugged-in parents of tweens and teens (Common Sense Media, California, 2017).

2. Wartella E., Rideout, V., Lauricella, A. Parenting in the Age of Digital Technology. http://cmhd.northwestern.edu/wp-content/uploads/2015/06/ParentingAgeDigital Technology.REVISED.FINAL_.2014.pdf. 2014.

3. "Cell Phone Addiction: The Statistics of Gadget Dependency," King University Online, https://online.king.edu/news/cell-phone-addiction/ July 27, 2017.

4. Radesky, J. et al. Maternal mobile device use during a structured parent-child interaction task. *Academy of Pediatrics.* 15, 238–244 (2015).

5. Oduor E., Neustaedter C., Odom W., Tang A., Moallem N., Tory M., et al. (eds.) The frustrations and benefits of mobile device usage in the home when co-present with family members. In Proc. of the 2016 ACM Conference on Designing Interactive Systems (ACM, New York, 2016)

6. Technoference: longitudinal associations between parent technology use, parenting stress, and child behavior problems, Brandon T. McDaniel and Jenny S. Radesky, Pediatric Research (2018) 84:210–218; https://doi.org/10.1038/s41390-018-0052-6

7. Jago R, Stamatakis E, Gama A, et al. Parent and child screen-viewing time and home media environment. *American Journal of Preventive Medicine.* (2012) 43(2):150–158.

8. AAP Council on Communications and Media. Media and Young Minds. *Pediatrics.* (2016) 138(5): e20162591.

9. Screen Time and Children, American Academy of Child and Adolescent Psychiatry, https://www.aacap.org/AACAP/Families_and_Youth/Facts_for_Families/FFF-Guide/Children-And-Watching-TV-054, February, 2020.

10. "To grow up healthy, children need to sit less and play more," World Health Organization, https://www.who.int/news/item/24-04-2019-to-grow-up-healthy-children-need-to-sit-less-and-play-more, April 24, 2019.

11. Screen Time and Children.

12. Megan, A. Moreno, M.D., "Media use for 5-to18-year-olds should reflect personalization, balance," AAP News, October 21, 2016.

13. AAP Council on Communications and Media. "Media Use in School-Age Children and Adolescents." *Pediatrics.* (2016) 138(5): e20162591.

14. Vedechkina Maria, Borgonovi Francesca, "A Review of Evidence on the Role of Digital Technology in Shaping Attention and Cognitive Control in Children," *Frontiers in Psychology*, Vol.12, 2021.

Chapter 1: Impact on Thinking and Learning

1. Jensen, Peter. *Journal of the Academy of Child and Adolescent Psychiatry*: 46. (December 1997).

2. Raz, A., and J. Buhle. "Typologies of Attentional Networks," *Nature Neuroscience*, 7: 367-379. (2006).

3. Ibid.

4. Anderson, D. R., et. al. *Watching Children Watch Television. Attention and Development of Cognitive Skills.* G. Hale and M. Lewis, eds. Publishing: 339. (1979).

5. Ibid., p. 370.

6. Kubey, Robert and Mihaly Csikszentmihalyi. *Television and the Quality of Life: How Viewing Shapes Everyday Experience.* Lawrence Erlbaum Associates: 139. (1990).

7. Zimmerman, Frederick J, PhD, Dimitri A. Christakis, MD, MPH, and Andrew N. Meltzoff, PhD. "Television and DVD/Video Viewing in Children Younger than 2 Years," *Archives of Pediatric and Adolescent Medicine*,161 (5): 473-479. (2007).

8. Christakis, DA, FJ Zimmerman, DL DiGiuseppe, CA McCarty. "Early television exposure and subsequent attentional problems in children," *Pediatrics*, 113: 708 –713. (2004).

9. Nathanson, A. I., Aladé, F., Sharp, M. L., Rasmussen, E. E., and Christy, K. "The relation between television exposure and executive function among preschoolers," *Developmental Psychology*. 50, 1497–1506. doi: 10.1037/a0035714. (2014).

10. Radesky, J., Chassiakos, Y. R., Ameenuddin, N., Navsaria, D., Ameenuddin, N., Boyd, R., et al. "Digital advertising to children," *Pediatrics* 146:20201681. doi: 10.1542/peds.2020-1681. (2020).

11. Tamana SK, Ezeugwu V, Chikuma J, Lefebvre DL, Azad MB, Moraes TJ, et al. "Screen-time is associated with inattention problems in preschoolers: Results from the CHILD birth cohort study," PLoS ONE 14(4): e0213995. https://doi.org/10.1371/journal.pone.0213995. (2019).

12. Gentile D. "Pathological Video-Game Use Among Youth Ages 8 to 18," *Journal of Psychological Science*, 3(2): 1-9. (2009).

13. Landhuis, CE, R Poulton, D Welch, RJ Hancox. "Does childhood television viewing lead to attention problems in adolescence? Results from a prospective longitudinal study," *Pediatrics*, 120: 532 –537. (2007).

14. Espiritu, Maya, "Early Childhood iPad Use and Effects on Visual Spatial Attention Span," Scripps Senior Theses. Paper 771. http://scholarship.claremont.edu/scripps_theses/771. (2016).

15. Swing, E.L., Gentile, D.A., Anderson, C.A., Walsh, D.A. "Television and Video Game Exposure and the Development of Attention Problems," *Pediatrics* Online 2010; 126, 214. (2010).

16. Swing, Edward Lee, "Plugged in: The effects of electronic media use on attention problems, cognitive control, visual attention, and aggression," Graduate Thesis, Iowa State University, (2012).

17. Vedechkina Maria, Borgonovi Francesca, "A Review of Evidence on the Role of Digital Technology in Shaping Attention and Cognitive Control in Children," *Frontiers in Psychology*, Vol.12, 2021.

18. Condry, John, *The Psychology of Television*. Lawrence Erlbaum Associates: 14. (1989).

19. Robinson, J. P. "Television's Impact on Everyday Life: Some Cross-National Evidence," *Television and Social Behavior*: Vol. 4. E. Rubinstein, G. Comstock, and J. P. Murray, eds. Government Printing Office: 410-431. (1972).

20. Corteen, R. S. "Television and Reading Skills," T. M. Williams. *The Impact of Television. A National Experiment Involving Three Communities*. Vancouver, B.C.: A symposium presented at the annual meeting of the Canadian Psychological Association, June 1977.

21. Condry, J. C. "Enemies of Exploration: Self-Initiated Versus Other-Initiated Learning," *Journal of Personality and Social Psychology*, 35 (7): 459-477. (1977).

22. Liza Hopkins, et.al., "Books, Bytes and Brains: The Implications of New Knowledge for Children's Early Literacy Learning," *Australasian Journal of Early Childhood* 38 (1):23-28 (2013).

23. Siibak, A., and Nevski, E. "Older siblings as mediators of infants' and toddlers' (digital) media use," in *The Routledge Handbook of Digital Literacies in Early Childhood*, eds O. Erstad, R. Flewitt, B. Kümmerling-Meibauer, and Í. Susana Pires Pere (Abingdon: Routledge), 123–133. (2019).

24. Orben, A. "The Sisyphean cycle of technology panics." *Perspectives in Psychological Science*, 14, 672–690. doi: 10.1177/1745691620919372. (2020).

25. Healy, Jane. *Endangered Minds*. Simon and Schuster: 97. (2005).

26. Pempek, Tiffany, Kirkorian, Heather L. & Anderson, Daniel R. "The Effects of Background Television on the Quantity and Quality of Child-Directed Speech by Parents," *Journal of Children and Media*, 8:3, 211-222, DOI: 10.1080/17482798.2014.920715. (2014).

27. Kirkorian, J., et. al. "The Impact of Background Television on Parent-Child Interaction." *Child Development*, 80 (5): 1350-1357. (2009).

28. Amanda C. Trofholz, Allan D. Tate, Michael H. Miner, Jerica M. Berge, "Associations between TV viewing at family meals and the emotional atmosphere of the meal, meal healthfulness, child dietary intake, and child weight status," *Appetite*, Volume 108, 2017.

29. Lapierre MA, Piotrowski JT, Linebarger DL. "Background television in the homes of US children." *Pediatrics*. 130(5):839-46. 2011-2581, Nov. 2012.

30. Konrad C, Hillmann M, Rispler J, Niehaus L, Neuhoff L, Barr R. "Quality of Mother-Child Interaction Before, During, and After Smartphone Use." *Frontier Psychololgy*.12:616656. March 29, 2021.

31. Braune-Krickau K, Schneebeli L, Pehlke-Milde J, Gemperle M, Koch R, von Wyl A. "Smartphones in the nursery: Parental smartphone use and parental sensitivity and responsiveness within parent-child interaction in early childhood (0-5 years): A scoping review." *Journal of Infant Mental Health*, 2021.

32. Horowitz-Kraus, T., DiFrancesco, M., Greenwood, P. et al. "Longer Screen Vs. Reading Time is Related to Greater Functional Connections Between the Salience Network and Executive Functions Regions in Children with Reading Difficulties Vs. Typical Readers," *Child Psychiatry and Human Development* 52, 681–692 (2021).

33. Veraksa Nikolay, Veraksa Aleksander, Gavrilova Margarita, Bukhalenkova Daria, Oshchepkova Ekaterina, Chursina Apollinaria, "Short- and Long-Term Effects of Passive and Active Screen Time on Young Children's Phonological Memory," *Frontiers in Education*, Vol. 6, 2021.

34. Lin, L. Y., Cherng, R. J., Chen, Y. J., Chen, Y. J., and Yang, H. M. "Effects of television exposure on developmental skills among young children." *Infant Behavior Development*. 38, 20–26. (2015).

35. Chonchaiya, W., and Pruksananonda, C. "Television viewing associates with delayed language development," *Acta Paediatrics*, (Olso, Norway) 97, 977–982. (2008).

36. Linebarger, D. L., and Walker, D. "Infants' and toddlers' television viewing and language outcomes," *American Behavioral Scientist.* 48, 624–645. (2005).

37. Christakis, D. A., Gilkerson, J., Richards, J. A., Zimmerman, F. J., Garrison, M. M., Xu, D., Gray, S. & Yapanel, U. "Audible Television and Decreased Adult Words, Infant Vocalizations, and Conversational Turns," *Archives of Pediatrics & Adolescent Medicine.* 163 (6):554-558. (2009).

38. Linebarger, D. L., Kosanic, A. Z., Greenwood, C. R., and Doku, N. S. "Effects of viewing the television program 'between the lions' on the emergent literacy skills of young children," *Journal of Educational Psychology.* 96, 297–308. doi: 10.1037/0022-0663.96.2.297 (2004).

39. Veraksa Nikolay, et.al., *Frontiers in Education*, Vol. 6, 2021.

40. Healy: 223.

41. Ibid.: 214

42. Condry: 160.

43. Ibid.: 162

44. Pagani, Linda S., et. al. "Prospective Associations Between Early Childhood Exposure and Academic, Psychosocial, and Physical Well-Being by Middle Childhood," *Archives of Pediatrics & Adolescent Medicine*, 164 (5): 450-467. (2010).

45. Armstrong, G.B., G.A. Boirsky, and M-L Mares. "Background Television and Reading Performance." *Communication Monographs*, 58, September (1991).

46. Huston, A. C., E. Donnerstein, H. Fairchild, N.D. Feshbach, P.A. Katz, J.P. Murray, E.A. Rubinstein, B.L. Wilcox, and D. Zuckerman. *Big World, Small Screen: The Role of Television in American Society.* Lincoln, Nebraska: University of Nebraska Press. (1992).

47. Christakis, D. et. al. 2004.

48. Dworak, Markus, Dipl Sportwiss, Thomas Schierl, Thomas Bruns, and Heiko Klaus Strüder. "Impact of Singular Excessive Computer Game and Television Exposure on Sleep Patterns and Memory Performance of School-aged Children." *Pediatrics*, Vol. 120 No. 5: 978-985, November (2007).

49. Rideout, Victoria, Donald Roberts, and Ulla Foehr. *Generation M: Media in the Lives of 8-18-Year-Olds.* Kaiser Family Foundation Study, March 2005.

50. Martins CMdL, Bandeira PFR, Lemos NBAG, Bezerra TA, Clark CCT, Mota J, Duncan MJ. "A Network Perspective on the Relationship between Screen Time, Executive Function, and Fundamental Motor Skills among Preschoolers," *International Journal of Environmental Research and Public Health.* 17(23):886, (2020).

51. Hutton JS, Dudley J, Horowitz-Kraus T, DeWitt T, Holland SK. "Associations Between Screen-Based Media Use and Brain White Matter Integrity in Preschool-Aged Children," *Journal of the American Medical Association Pediatrics.* 174(1):e193869. (2020).

52. Lillard AS, Li H, Boguszewski K. "Television and children's executive function," *Advancements in Child Development and Behavior.* 48:219-248. (2015).

53. Zivan M, Bar S, Jing X, Hutton J, Farah R, Horowitz-Kraus T. "Screen-exposure and altered brain activation related to attention in preschool children: An EEG study," Trends *Neuroscience Education.* 17:1-5. (2019).

54. Nathanson AI, Aladé F, Sharp ML, Rasmussen EE, Christy K. "The relation between television exposure and executive function among preschoolers," *Developmental Psychology*. 50(5):1497-1506. (2014).

55. Jennifer Cross, MD, "What Does too Much Screen Time do to Kids' Brains?" *Health Matters*, 2019, https://healthmatters.nyp.org/what-does-too-much-screen-time-do-to-childrens-brains/

56. *Screen Time and Children*, American Academy of Child and Adolescent Psychiatry, https://www.aacap.org/AACAP/Families_and_Youth/Facts_for_Families/FFF-Guide/Children-And-Watching-TV-054, February, 2020.

57. "Survey Shows Parents Alarmed as Kids' Screen Time Skyrockets During COVID-19 Crisis," Parents Together Foundation Survey, https://parents-together.org/survey-shows-parents-alarmed-as-kids-screen-time-skyrockets-during-covid-19-crisis/ April 23, 2020.

58. "The Association between Screen Engagement and Children's Developing Brains," *Children and Screens*, Nov. 3, 2021.

59. Singh, Kunsh and Molloy, Karen, "The Changes of Cognition in Teenagers after Playing Video Games," *Journal of Student Research*, August, 2021.

60. Adelantado-Renau M, Moliner-Urdiales D, Cavero-Redondo I, Beltran-Valls MR, Martínez-Vizcaíno V, Álvarez-Bueno C. "Association Between Screen Media Use and Academic Performance Among Children and Adolescents: A Systematic Review and Meta-analysis," *Journal of American Medical Association Pediatrics*. (2019).

61. Park, H., Kim, H.S., & Park, H.W. "A scientometric study of digital literacy, ICT literacy, information literacy, and media literacy," *Journal of Data and Information Science*, 6 (2), 116–138, (2021).

62. Jenny Radesky, Yolanda (Lind Reid Chassiakos, Nusheen Ameenuddin, Dipesh Navsaria, "Digital Advertising to Children," Council on Communication and Media, *Pediatrics*, 146, July 2020.

63. Ibid.

64. Singer, D. and J. Singer. *The House of Make Believe: Children's Play and the Developing Imagination*. Harvard University Press: 183. (1990).

65. Singer, J. and D. Singer. *Television, Imagination, and Aggression: A Study of Pre-Schoolers*. Lawrence Erlbaum Associates: 152. (1981).

66. Valkenburg, P., & van der Voort, T. H. A. "The influence of television on children's daydreaming styles: A 1-year panel study." *Communication Research*, 22, 267–287, (1995).

67. Pearce, Joseph Chilton. *Evolution's End: Claiming the Potential of Our Intelligence*. Harper Books: 165-166. (1992).

68. Damasio, Antonio. *The Feeling of What Happens: Body and Emotion in the Making of Consciousness*, Harcourt Brace and Company, 318. (1999).

69. Csikszentmihalyi, Mihaly. *Flow: The Psychology of Optimal Experience*, Harper and Row, 128 (1990).

70. Sanders, Barry. *A is for Ox: The Collapse of Literacy and the Rise of Violence in an Electronic Age*. Vintage Books: 93. (1994).

71. Ennemoser, M., & Schneider, W. "Relations of television viewing and reading: Findings from a 4-year longitudinal study," *Journal of Educational Psychology*, 99, 349–368. (2007).

72. Weis, R., & Cerankosky, B. C. "Effects of video-game ownership on young boys' academic and behavioral functioning: A randomized, controlled study," *Psychological Science*, 21, 463–470. (2010).

73. Glenberg, A., Brown, M., & Levin, J. "Enhancing comprehension in small reading groups using a manipulation strategy," *Contemporary Educational Psychology*, 32, 389–399. (2007).

74. Wallace, C. E., & Russ, S. W. "Pretend play, divergent thinking, and math achievement in girls: A longitudinal study," *Psychology of Aesthetics, Creativity, and the Arts*, 9, 296–305. (2015).

75. Suggate, S.P., Martzog P., "Screen-time influences children's mental imagery performance," *Developmental Science*, e12978. (2020).

76. *Evolution's End: Claiming the Potential of Our Intelligence*, 167-168.

77. Martzog, P., & Suggate, S. "Fine motor skills and mental imagery: Is it all in the mind?" *Journal of Experimental Child Psychology*, 186, 59–72. (2019).

78. Ibid., Suggate and Martzog, 2020.

79. Valkenburg, P., & Peter, J. "Five challenges for the future of media-effects research," *International Journal of Communication*, 7,197–215. (2013).

80. Lillard, A. S., & Peterson, J. "The immediate impact of different types of television on young children's executive function," *Pediatrics*, 128, 644–649. (2011).

81. Nikkelen, S. W. C., Valkenburg, P., Huizinga, M., & Bushman, B. J. "Media use and ADHD-related behaviors in children and adolescents: A meta-analysis." *Developmental Psychology*, 50, 2228–2241. (2014).

82. Christakis, Dimitri. "Formal features of touchscreen apps may induce compulsive use in toddlers," *Journal of the American Academy of Child and Adolescent Psychiatry*, 60 (10), S297-S298, October 2021.

83. Yolanda (Linda) Reid Chassiakos, Jenny Radesky, Dimitri Christakis, Megan A. Moreno, Corinn Cross. "Children and Adolescents and Digital Media," Council on Communications and Media, *Pediatrics*, 138. (2016).

84. Fox Matthew, *Creativity: Where the Divine and the Human Meet*, Jeremy P. Tarcher/Putnam, 59-60. (2007).

85. Ibid., Csikszentmihalyi, Mihaly, 16.

86. Quoted by Conrad Kottak in: *Prime-Time Society: An Anthropological Analysis of Television and Culture*. Wadsworth Publishing: 10. (1990).

87. Fine, Sean. "Early fascination with reading gives way to computers, television as early as Grade 3," *Globe and Mail*: A-9. March 15, 2001.

88. Ibid.

89. Adelantado-Renau, Mireia, et.al. September (2019).

90. Bettelheim, Bruno. *A Good Enough Parent: A Book on Child Rearing*. Vintage Books: 177. (1987).

Chapter 2: Impact on Feelings and Behavior

1. Mander, Jerry, *Four Arguments for the Elimination of Television*, Harper Collins, (1978).

2. Christakis, DA, FJ Zimmerman, DL DiGiuseppe, CA McCarty. "Early television exposure and subsequent attentional problems in children," *Pediatrics*, 113: 708 –713. (2004).

3. DeGaetano, Gloria and Kathleen Bander. *Screen Smarts: A Family Guide to Media Literacy*, Houghton Mifflin: 57. (1996).

4. Tamana, Sukhpreet, et. al., "Screen-Time is associated with inattention problems in preschoolers: Results from the CHILD birth cohort study," *Plos One*, April 17, 2019.

5. Neitz, Ross, "Too much screen time associated with behavior problems in preschoolers," University of Alberta, Faculty of Medicine and Dentistry, April 17, 2019.

6. Barr, Rachel and Linebarger, Deborah, eds., *Media Exposure During Infancy and Early Childhood: The Effects of Content and Context on Learning and Development*, Springer International Publishing, p. xiii, (2017).

7. Christakis, Dimitri, "Formal features of touchscreen apps may induce compulsive use in toddlers," *Journal of the American Academy of Child and Adolescent Psychiatry*, 60 (10): S 297-S298, October 2021.

8. McArthur, Brae Anne, "Cumulative social risk and child screen use: the role of child temperament," *Journal of Pediatric Psychology*, jsab087, August, 13, 2021.

9. Wilmer, H.H., Chein, J.M., "Mobile technology habits: patterns of association among device usage, intertemporal preference, impulse control, and reward sensitivity," *Psychonomic Bulletin & Review*, 23, 1607–1614. (2016).

10. Plante, Courtney, et. al., *Game On! Sensible Answers about Video Games and Media Violence*, Zengen LLC: 352. (2020.)

11. Gathercoal, Paul. "Brain Research and Mediated Experience: An Interpretation of the Implications for Education," *Clearinghouse* 63: 271. February (1990).

12. Lembke, Anna, M.D., "Digital Addictions are Drowning Us in Dopamine," *Wall Street Journal*, August 14, 2021.

13. Grossman, Dave and Gloria DeGaetano. *Stop Teaching Our Kids to Kill: A Call to Action Against TV, Movie, and Video Game Violence*. Harmony Books: 69. (2014).

14. Ibid., 86-87.

15. Plante, Courtney, et. al., 96.

16. Grossman, Dave and Gloria DeGaetano., 37.

17. Ibid., 38.

18. Ibid.

19. Plante, Courtney, et. al., 96.

20. Anderson, C. A., Shibuya, A., Ihori, N., Swing, E. L., Bushman, B. J., Sakamoto, A., Saleem, M., "Violent video game effects on aggression, empathy, and prosocial behavior in eastern and western countries: A meta-analytic review," *Psychological Bulletin*, 136, 151–173. (2010).

21. George Gerbner and Nancy Signorielli, *Violence Profile, 1976 Through 1988-89" Enduring Patterns*, manuscript, University of Pennsylvania, Annenberg School of Communication. (1990).

22. Joanne Cantor, "Media and fear in children and adolescents," in *Media Violence and Children*, ed. Douglas A. Gentile, Prager, 187. (2003).

23. Grossman, Dave and Gloria DeGaetano., 60-62.

24. Ibid., 63.

25. Ibid.

26. Jeanne Funk, "Children's exposure to violent video games and desensitization to violence," *Child and Adolescent Psychiatry*, vol. 14. no. 3: 402. July, 2006.

27. Grossman, Dave and Gloria DeGaetano., 67.

28. Ibid., 26.

29. Grossman and DeGaetano. 2014. Citing Eron and Huesman: 51.

30. Centerwall, Brandon, M. D., "Television and Violence: The Scale of the Problem and Where to Go from Here." *Journal of the American Medical Association*: 3,059, June 10, 1992.

31. Pew Research Center. *Teens, Social Media, and Technology*. (2018).

32. Uhls Y.A., Michikyan M., Morris J., Garcia, D., Small G.W, Zgourou E., Greenfield P.M. "Five days at outdoor education camp without screens improves preteen skills with nonverbal emotion cues." *Computers in Human Behavior*, Volume 39, 387–392, October 2014.

33. Wolpert, Stuart. "In our digital world, are young people losing the ability to read emotions?" *UCLA Newsroom*, August, 21, 2014.

34. Johnson, K. J., Waugh, C. E., & Fredrickson, B. L. "Smile to see the forest: Facially expressed positive emotions broaden cognition." *Cognition and Emotion*, 24(2), 299–321, (2010).

35. Bruner quote in: DeGaetano, Gloria. *Television and the Lives of Our Children*. Train of Thought Publishing: 33. 1996.

36. "Best Fort Ever," Recreational Equipment, Inc., Fall Catalog. (2021).

37. Turkel Sherry, *Alone Together: Why We Expect More from Technology and Less from Each Other*, Basic Books, 2011.

38. Turner, Richard, M.D., "How screen time affects the parent-child relationship," Margaret Mary Health, June 7, 2019.

39. Kildare, Cory and Middlemiss, Wendy, "Impact of parents mobile device use on parent-child interaction," *Computers in Human Behavior*, October 2017.

40. Arredondo, D. E. & Leonard, H. "Attachment, bonding, and reciprocal connectedness." *Journal of the Center for Families, Children, & the Courts*, 2, 109-127. (2000).

41. Kotulak, Ronald. *Inside the Brain*. Andrews McNeel Publishing: 39. (1997).

42. Heintz-Knowles, Katharine. "The reflections of the screen: televisions' image of children," *Children Now Study*: 5, February 1995.

43. Nelson, P. "Digital neural-amplification: paranoia and digital media." *Academia Letter*, Article 3682, October 2021.

44. Dill-Shackelford, Karen, PhD., *How Fantasy Becomes Reality: Information & Entertainment media in Everyday Life*. Oxford University Press. (2016).

45. Dill-Shackelford, Karen, PhD. et.al., "Social Group Stories in the Media and Child Development." *Pediatrics*, Volume 140, number s2, November, 2017.

Chapter 3: Impact on General Health and Well-Being

1. Dietz WH, Jr., Gortmaker SL. "Do we fatten our children at the television set? Obesity and television viewing in children and adolescents," *Pediatrics*, 75:807-12, 1985.

2. "Pediatrics Group Urges Ban on TV Food Ads for Kids," *Deseret News*, July 23, 1991.

3. Zimmerman FJ, Bell JF. "Associations of television content type and obesity in children." *American Journal of Public Health*, 100:334-40, (2010).

4. Harvard T.C. Chan School of Public Health, On-line Obesity Prevention Source, https://www.hsph. harvard.edu/obesity-prevention-source/obesity-causes/television-and-sedentary-behavior-and-obesity/

5. O'Brien M, Nader PR, Houts, RM, Bradley R, Friedman SL, Belsky J, Susman E., "The ecology of childhood overweight: a 12-year longitudinal analysis," *International Journal of Obesity*, 31(9):1469-78, September, 2007.

6. Rey-López JP, Vicente-Rodríguez G, Biosca M, Moreno, LA., "Sedentary behavior and obesity development in children and adolescents," *Nutrition, Metabolism and Cardiovascular Diseases* (3) 242-51, March 18, 2007.

7. Boone JE, Gordon-Larsen P, Adair LS, Popkin BM, "Screen time and physical activity during adolescence: longitudinal effects on obesity in young adulthood," *International Journal of Behavioral Nutrition and Physical Activity*, 4:26, June 8, 2007.

8. Erik Landhuis, Poulton R, Welch D, Hancox RJ, "Programming obesity and poor fitness: the long-term impact of childhood television." *Obesity* 16(6):1457-9, June 2008.

9. Parsons TJ, Manor O, Power C., "Television viewing and obesity: a prospective study in the 1958 British birth cohort." *European Journal of Clinician Nutrition*, 62(12):1355-63, December 2008.

10. Mendoza, Jason A., Fred J. Zimmerman, and Dimitri A. Christakis. "Television viewing, computer use, obesity, and adiposity in US preschool children," *International Journal of Behavioral Nutrition and Physical Activity*, 4: 44, September 25, 2007.

11. Laurson RK, M.S., JC Eisenmann, Ph.D., GJ Welk, Ph.D., EE Wickel, Ph.D., DA Gentile, Ph.D., and DA Walsh, Ph.D., "Combined influence of physical activity and screen time recommendations on childhood overweight," *The Journal of Pediatrics*, 10.1016 (2008).

12. Engberg, Elina, et. Al., "Heavy screen users are the heaviest among 10,000 children," *Scientific Reports*, (2019).

13. Fang, Kehong, et. Al., "Screen time and childhood overweight/obesity: A systematic review and meta-analysis," *Child: Care, Health, and Development*, July 2019.

14. Robinson, Thomas N., M. Wilde, L. Navacruz, et. al., "Effects of reducing children's television and video game use on aggressive behavior: a randomized controlled trial," *Archives of Pediatric Medicine*. 155: 17-23. (2001).

15. Hrafbkelsdottir, Sofia, et.al., "Less screen time and more frequent vigorous physical activity is associated with lower risk of reporting negative mental health symptoms among Icelandic adolescents." *Plos One*, April 26, 2018.

16. Tandon PS, Zhou C, Johnson AM, Gonzalez ES, Kroshus E., "Association of Children's Physical Activity and Screen Time with Mental Health During the COVID-19 Pandemic," *Journal of the American Medical Association*, 4(10) (2021).

17. Wilmer and Chein, (2016)

18. Ibid.

19. Michelle D. Guerrero, Joel D. Barnes, Jeremy J. Walsh, Jean-Philippe Chaput, Mark S. Tremblay and Gary S. Goldfield, "24-Hour Movement Behaviors and Impulsivity," *Pediatrics*: 144, (2019).

20. Gardener, J. and S. Fitzpatrick, et. al., "Families who eat dinner together with the television off eat more fruits and vegetables than those who eat separately or with the television on," *Journal of the American Dietetic Association*. April 2007.

21. Martinez-Gomez, David, Jared Tucker, Kate A. Heelan, Gregory J. Welk, and Joey C. Eisenmann, "Associations Between Sedentary Behavior and Blood Pressure in Young Children." *Archives of Pediatric Adolescent Medicine*, 163(8): 724-730. (2009).

22. Lissak G., "Adverse physiological and psychological effects of screen time on children and adolescents: Literature review and case study," *Environmental Resources*, 164:149-157, July 2018.

23. Ibid.

24. Hirshkowitz M, Whiton K, Albert SM, Alessi C, Bruni O, DonCarlos L, Hazen N, Herman J, Katz ES, Kheirandish-Gozal L, Neubauer DN, O'Donnell AE, Ohayon M, Peever J, Rawding R, Sachdeva RC, Setters B, Vitiello MV, Ware JC, Adams Hillard PJ., "National Sleep Foundation's sleep time duration recommendations: methodology and results summary," *Sleep Health*, (1):40-43, March 1, 2015.

25. Lauren Hale, Stanford Guan, "Screen time and sleep among school-aged children and adolescents: A systematic literature review," *Sleep Medicine Reviews*, Volume 21, (2015).

26. Pernilla Garmy, Eva K. Clausson, Per Nyberg, Ulf Jakobsson, "Insufficient Sleep Is Associated with Obesity and Excessive Screen Time Amongst Ten-Year-Old Children in Sweden," *Journal of Pediatric Nursing*, Volume 39, (2018).

27. Buchner, Jill, "Touchscreens are bad for toddlers' and babies' sleep," *Today's Parent*, April 17, 2017.

28. Hale, Lauren, et al. "Youth Screen Media Habits and Sleep: Sleep-Friendly Screen Behavior Recommendations for Clinicians, Educators, and Parents," *Child and Adolescent Psychiatric Clinics of North America*, vol. 27, 2: 229-245 (2018).

29. Kiran P. Maski, Sanjeev V. Kothare, "Sleep deprivation and neurobehavioral functioning in children," *International Journal of Psychophysiology*, Volume 89, Issue 2, 259-264, (2013).

30. Hale, et. al.

31. Guerrero, Michelle, Ph.D., "Impulsive Behavior Linked to Sleep and Screen Time," *Healthy Active Living and Research Group*, University of Ottawa, August 14, 2019.

32. Ma M, Xiong S, Zhao S, Zheng Z, Sun T, Li C., "COVID-19 Home Quarantine Accelerated the Progression of Myopia in Children Aged 7 to 12 Years in China," *Investigative Ophthalmology & Visual Science*, 62: August 2, 2021.

33. Foreman, Joshua, et. al., "Association between digital smart device use and myopia: a systematic review and meta-analysis," *Lancet Digital Health*, October 5, 2021.

34. Distefano, Linda, "Plano Today Publishes Global Evidence Linking Time Spent in Front of A Digital Device To Myopia (Myopia) in The Lancet Digital Health," Automatic Link Exchange, October 5, 2021. https://automatic-link-exchange.com/plano-today-publishes-global-evidence-linking-time-spent-in-front-of-a-digital-device-to-myopia-myopia-in-the-lancet-digital-health/

35. Twenge, Jean M.; et al., "Increases in Depressive Symptom, Suicide-Related Outcomes, and Suicide Rates Among U.S. Adolescents after 2010 and Links to Increased New Media Screen Time," *Clinical Psychological Science*, January 2018.

36. Mercado MC, Holland K, Leemis RW, Stone DM, Wang J., "Trends in Emergency Department Visits for Nonfatal Self-inflicted Injuries Among Youth Aged 10 to 24 Years in the United States," 2001-2015. 318(19):1931–1933, *Journal of the American Medical Association*, (2017).

37. Haidt, Jonathan, "The Dangerous Experiment on Teen Girls," *Atlantic Monthly*, Nov. 21, 2021.

38. Shuai, Lan., "Influences of digital media use on children and adolescents with ADHD during COVID-10 pandemic," *Global Health*,17 (1):48, April 19, 2021.

39. Lissak, Gadi, "Adverse physiological and psychological effects of screen time on children and adolescents: Literature review and case study," *Environmental Resources*, 164:149-157, July 2018.

40. Gunnell, Katie E., et. al., "Examining the bidirectional relationship between physical activity, screen time, and symptoms of anxiety and depression over time during adolescence," *Preventive Medicine,* Volume 88, 147-152, (2016).

41. Wang, X., Li, Y. & Fan, H., "The associations between screen time-based sedentary behavior and depression: a systematic review and meta-analysis," *BMC Public Health*, 19, 1524 (2019).

42. Bell, Courtney, et.al., "An Overview of Research on the Impact that Viewing Pornography has on Children, Pre-Teens, and Teenagers," *Bravehearts Foundation Limited*, July 2017.

43. Dines, Gail, Ph.D., Fact Sheet, Culture Re-Framed Website, December, 2021. https://www.culturere-framed.org/wp-content/uploads/2019/08/CR-At-A-Glance.pdf

44. Ibid.

45. Parents Television and Media Council, "This New Data About Children is Heartbreaking…and Infuriating!" Online Blog, December, 6, 2021. https://www.parentstv.org/blog/this-new-data-about-children-is-heartbreaking-and-infuriating?fbclid=IwAR27m3TlzU57nd-6pVa-l-ouJYAS_mAKUXRPgFFS6i-HvXHjdVV5D2pun8Rc

46. Ibid.

47. Dines, Culture Re-Framed website.

48. Parents Television and Media Council Online blog.

49. Dines, Gail, Ph.D., Fact Sheet, Culture Re-Framed Website.

50. Parents Television and Media Council Online blog.

51. Wright, P. J., "Mass media effects on youth sexual behavior assessing the claim for causality," *Annals of the International Communication Association*, 35(1), 343-385, (2011).

52. Smith, L. W., Liu, B., Degenhardt, L., Richters, J., Patton, G., Wand, H., Cross, D., Hocking, J. S., Skinner, R. S., Cooper, S., Lumby, C., Kaldor, J. M., & Guy, R., "Is sexual content in new media linked to sexual risk behavior in young people? A systematic review and meta-analysis." *Sexual Health*, 13, 501-515, (2016).

53. van Oosten, J. M. F., Peter, J., & Vandenbosch, L., "Adolescents' sexual media use and willingness to engage in casual sex: Differential relations and underlying processes." *Human Communication Research*, 43(1), 127-147, (2017).

54. Wright, P. J., et. al., "A Meta-Analysis of Pornography Consumption and Actual Acts of Sexual Aggression in General Population," *Studies Journal of Communication*, Dec. 2015.

55. "Brain Studies of Porn Users and Sex Addicts," Your Brian on Porn website: https://www.yourbrainon-porn.com/relevant-research-and-articles-about-the-studies/brain-studies-on-porn-users-sex-addicts/

56. Haney, John, "Teenagers and Pornography Addiction: Treating the Silent Epidemic," Vistas Online: https://www.counseling.org/docs/default-source/vistas/teenagers-and-pornography-addiction-treat-ing-the-silent-epidemic.pdf?sfvrsn=8

57. Ansari, Maria, "Survey revels more than 40 percent of children are chatting with strangers," Wave News, September 10, 2019.

58. Dines, Gail, Ph.D., Fact Sheet, Culture Re-Framed Website

59. "It's Normal to Talk to Randoms Online, Kids, Say," Family Zone Blog, 2021. https://www.familyzone.com/anz/families/blog/its-normal-to-talk-to-randoms-online

60. Ibid.

61. Kottak, Conrad, *Prime-Time Society*. Wadsworth Publishing, (1990).

62. Doornwaard, S. M., Bickham, D. S., Rich, M., Vanwesenbeeck, I., van den Eijnden, R. J. J. M., & ter Bogt, T. F. M., "Sex-related online behaviors and adolescents' body and sexual self perceptions," *Pediatrics*, 134(6), 1103-1110, December, 2014.

63. Folkvord, F., et.al., "Children's bonding with popular YouTube vloggers and their attitudes toward brand and product endorsements in vlogs: an explorative study," *Young Consumers*, Vol. 20, No. 2, (2019).

64. "15-Year-Old Dies from 'Choking Challenge' on Instagram," CBS News December 8, 2021. https://www.cbsnews.com/video/instagram-ceo-testifies-congress-social-media-impact-on-teen-users/?int-cid=CNM-00 10abd1h&fbclid=IwAR3JRNXjAdkVbMbrFePW1i3RsS5rIobcSdO39dP7mh_4YkxyzS-LL7_EXjos#x

65. Katz, S., et.al., "Predicting Parent-Child Differences in Perceptions of How Children Use the Internet for Help With Homework, Identity Development, and Health Information," *Journal of Broadcasting & Electronic Media*, 59:4, 574-602, (2015).

66. "Our Sacred Hearts," Richard Rohr's Daily Meditation, December, 17, 2021.

About the Author

Gloria DeGaetano, (www.GloriaDeGaetano.com) an internationally acclaimed educator and parent coach, is the author of several books and manuals to help moms and dads parent well in technological times. She is the founder and CEO of the Parent Coaching Institute (PCI) (www.thePCI.org), a global company offering Parent Coach Certification® for family professionals, coaching services for parents, and specialized programs for companies and organizations. An educator with varied experiences—as a classroom teacher, school district administrator, university instructor, and international consultant —she brings a wide range of expertise to her coaching work with parents and her training of professional parent coaches. She is the mother of two adult sons and lives with her husband in Bellingham, WA—a poster city for the beautiful Pacific Northwest.

www.ingramcontent.com/pod-product-compliance
Lightning Source LLC
Chambersburg PA
CBHW080848120626
46553CB00009B/2624